FORM AND CONTENT
IN THE
CHRISTIAN TRADITION

A FRIENDLY DISCUSSION

BETWEEN

W. SANDAY, D.D.
LADY MARGARET PROFESSOR AND CANON OF CHRIST CHURCH

AND

N. P. WILLIAMS, M.A.
CHAPLAIN-FELLOW OF EXETER COLLEGE

WIPF & STOCK · Eugene, Oregon

Wipf and Stock Publishers
199 W 8th Ave, Suite 3
Eugene, OR 97401

Form and Content in the Christian Tradition
A Friendly Discussion Between W. Sanday and N. P. Williams
By Sanday, William and Williams, N. P.
Softcover ISBN-13: 978-1-6667-3501-7
Hardcover ISBN-13: 978-1-6667-9160-0
eBook ISBN-13: 978-1-6667-9161-7
Publication date 9/15/2021
Previously published by Longmans, Green, and Co., 1916

This edition is a scanned facsimile of the original edition published in 1916.

PREFACE

IT should be explained at the outset that the discussion which follows is quite independent of another which I believe will be published in the same external style and at the same time. I happen to be personally a connecting link between the two discussions, and the outward form which they have assumed follows naturally from the subject-matter. But the occasions which gave rise to them are wholly distinct, and the fact that both give expression to views opposed to mine must not be taken to imply any further concert or alliance between my critics. There are really three positions indicated, each of which must stand upon its own merits.

The present discussion arose out of an article contributed by me to *The Modern Churchman* for June 1915, and I am indebted to the editor for permission to reprint it. It had been read just before as an address at a meeting of the Churchmen's Union. The article was written for this meeting under some pressure, and I am afraid rather less quietly than might have been wished. But it seemed right to reprint it practically as it stood because it was in this form that it lay before Mr. Williams; and there may perhaps be some increase in frankness and clearness to set against the fault of over-emphasis. The further course of the discussion will explain itself.

We agreed between ourselves that, as the writer of the concluding paper had the last word in the body of the book, the writer of the Preface should have a limited right of final reply, just to remove misunderstandings and to wind up the discussion on any point that might need it. I think I can promise not to abuse this privilege.

I can do so the more easily because, although Mr. Williams has in one or two places rather misunderstood me and in the course of his argument ascribed to me ideas which I am far from holding, he has yet in the main represented my views with conspicuous fairness and often with a lucidity for which I am specially grateful to him. I often prefer his mode of statement to my own. In saying this I ought perhaps to add that, where alternative views are attributed to me (as e. g. on pp. 123, 128) it would, I think, always be safe for the reader to assume that the more moderate and reasonable view is that which I should adopt.

I am sanguine that our discussion as a whole—whatever may be its effect, or want of effect, upon opinion—will have at least served the chief purpose for which it was undertaken : that of making the two positions stand out clearly before the public mind. Where this has been done, it may be understood that I shall not make any further comment simply for the sake of making comment. There are, however, in the last paper just a few points that still need clearing up in respect to (1) the nature of veracity (§ I, pp. 119–21) ; (2) the historical method (§§ II, III, pp. 121–5); (3) miracles (§§ IV–XVII, pp. 125–44); (4) relativity of expression (§§ XVIII–XXVI, pp. 145–67). To these I will now ask leave to address myself.

(1) (§ I, pp. 119–21). I was far from wishing to impute to Mr. Williams any ' indifference to truth ' in the common acceptation of the term. The real difference between us is a difference in the definition of truth, especially in relation to authority. I think I understand Mr. Williams's motive in the acceptance of authority ; and I should be quite willing to give it a good name—such as ' loyalty ' or the like. But I should not naturally, in my own use of

words, call the result obtained exactly 'truth', because it would not to my mind possess all the marks or criteria of truth that I should consider necessary. It is well known that the definition of truth is still a moot point among philosophers. I suspect that I should not see eye to eye with Mr. Williams in this respect. But I do not want to assume that I am right and he is wrong.

(2) (§§ II, III, pp. 121–5). In regard to the application of modern historical methods, I should wish to tone down slightly some of the expressions that Mr. Williams has used in the statement of my views ('a degree of efficiency and certitude hitherto undreamed of'; 'complete *bouleversement* of the traditional view'; 'mathematical certainty'). Indeed I should imagine that he might, on second thoughts, apply the same process with advantage to the paragraphs in which he states his own position ('entirely dispute'; 'jettison beliefs'; 'consciously aim at producing a *bouleversement* of New Testament tradition'). These are just little exuberances of expression which I only deprecate because I do not wish to give the idea that the results of modern methods are more certain than they are. They profess only to be approximate and not exact. My main point is that the same methods must be applied in precisely the same way to the New Testament as to the Old. I do not propose to assume that the result will necessarily be the same; though I believe that, where the conditions are similar, it is likely to be. There are two further conditions, one telling one way and the other the other. The first is that there will be in the different cases different degrees of attestation—which may be presumed to be on the whole in favour of the New Testament tradition. But, to set against this, is the fact that the New Testament writers and trans-

mitters had the Old Testament before them and were liable to be influenced by it in the direction of assimilating the one set of narratives to the other.

I may at this point bring in a reference to what is said on pp. 142–4. While admitting in general terms that the attestation of the New Testament is in the main superior to that of the Old, I am afraid I could not admit that it was in any one of the disputed cases so superior as to be decisive. It should be remembered that the points in debate do not in any case cover the whole of a complex incident; they only affect particular features of it. And, so far as these particular features are concerned, I should certainly maintain that the evidence was insufficient to establish them. That is a point to which I have given some study, and I am not speaking at random. I have said that the very best New Testament evidence—the evidence of St. Paul's Epistles to the experiences of the Apostle himself—is in none of these instances available. Two of them depend on the witness of St. Luke alone, in parts of his writings which do not possess the highest authority. These—when applied, as I have just said, to a detail and not to a whole incident—would not be enough in themselves to sustain it even if it had been in itself perfectly unexceptionable. Still less can they bear the weight of the features for which they are alleged. No doubt there is a graduated scale of documents. But there is only one of the debated points for which the evidence can be described as really strong.

This one point is in the Feeding of the Multitude, of which we have two versions. But it should be remembered that I only challenge a single detail in this incident. That something like it happened, I have no doubt. I quite believe that there was a meal, which was in some way made a sacred meal. All that I doubt is that it satisfied the hunger of four or five thousand men. My belief is that this one detail came in through the influence of an Old Testament parallel. I allow that the narrative must have assumed something very like its present shape at a relatively early date—not later, I should say, than the decade A.D. 50–60. But if we consider the mental attitude of those by whom it was transmitted, that seems to me quite possible. We have seen strange things rapidly come to be believed in our own time. I will return to the question of the clauses in the Creed before I have done.

(3) (§§ IV–XVII, pp. 125–44). At the outset of what is said about Miracles there is a momentary lapse, not only from accurate representation but (I must needs think) from clearness of thinking. I willingly accept the substitution of 'the laws of physics and chemistry' for 'the laws of matter and motion'. But it is a very different thing to say that certain alleged events must not 'contradict' these laws and to say that they must be wholly explicable by them. I should never have dreamed of saying anything of the kind. It would be as much opposed to my theory of the universe as it is to that of Mr. Williams. I am relieved from the necessity of dwelling upon this, because § VII is a complete and satisfactory answer to § VI. I have nothing to add to it.

When I speak of a 'breach' or 'contradiction' of the laws of physics and chemistry, I mean something inconsistent with those laws, something which treats them as if they were not valid. The argument which Mr. Williams directs against me in § IX is one that I have dealt with at some length in another place. It happens that I made use of the same illustration—the catching of a ball—to illustrate the difference between what I believe to be tenable and what is not. Incidentally, it illustrates also what I mean by a cause *supra naturam*.

There is no better example of such a cause than that of personal initiative, the introduction of spirit and will. The broad line which I took was that we have examples all round us on the largest possible scale of the operation of this kind of cause. We can see what kind of effect it has upon the lower laws of matter and motion (or physics and chemistry). I pointed out that these effects are themselves in turn subject to laws, or rather to certain regular limitations. The action of spirit or mind constantly overrides, controls and deflects, the lower laws of matter. But, while it does this, it never 'contradicts' them. The interaction of spirit and matter is a definite sphere to itself. But it too is a cosmos and not a chaos. It has laws of its own which are just as fixed in their way as the lower laws of physics and chemistry. There is always a special process of adjustment which prevents any real breach in the order of nature. Nature (i. e. these lower phenomena in nature) is controlled and regulated by spirit; but this very control is itself subject to rules and limitations: *naturae non nisi parendo imperatur.* Mind is superior to matter, but its superiority is exercised constitutionally, and not despotically. Laws of the lower order are overruled, but they are never violated.

This holds good for all the infinite variety of cases in which there is contact and influence passing to and fro from mind to matter and from matter to mind. The human will exerts an astonishing amount of power in its way; but it never fails to *respect* the appropriate laws of that with which it deals. And, as far as our experience goes, what is true of the human will is equally true of the Divine Will. It too, so far as we can see, works through and in accordance with the laws which it has itself laid down. But if it does so in the present, the presumption is that it has done so equally in the past. Our contention is that the handful of alleged cases in which it is supposed to have done otherwise is not enough to prove the contrary. This handful of alleged cases is far more easily and naturally explained in other ways.

That, as Mr. Williams rightly sees, is the ground that I wish really to take up. He quotes another example (besides the cricket ball) to which I happen to have given particular attention. The story of the Flood, he says, has been definitely disproved. 'But nobody has ever proved, or presumably ever will be able to prove (in the sense of rigorously certain demonstration), that Elisha did *not* make the iron to swim' (p. 141). No; the story of Elisha and the axe-head has not been disproved 'in the sense of rigorously certain demonstration'. But it is very easily—and I cannot help thinking, satisfactorily—explained. It is well known that the waters of the Dead Sea are so impregnated with salt that their specific gravity is considerably higher than that of ordinary water. I do not know whether iron will float in the Dead Sea or not; but in any case objects that would sink in other waters would not sink in these. If a dweller on the central ridge of Palestine had occasion to visit the shore of the Dead Sea, he might easily see a phenomenon of this kind, and (in Elisha's day) he would naturally regard it as a miracle. There would thus arise a class of miracle of this kind; and the nameless author of the story (not to be identified with the writer of the narrative, and perhaps not more than half conscious of what he was doing) would have plenty of precedent to fall back upon. The Leprosy of Gehazi may, I believe, be explained in a very similar way. I have myself heard a well-authenticated story of a sudden mental shock, under certain pathological conditions, causing a violent outbreak of eczema. An ancient, who was also not an expert, would not distinguish this from leprosy. And if an incident of this kind happened, not only would there be a miracle, but a class of miracles would be set up that might be drawn upon indefinitely.

These are just instances of the old-fashioned rationalism, which no doubt was invoked more often than it should have been, but which certainly had in it a considerable element of truth. We have learnt in these days not to trust too much to any one mode of explanation. A wise man will not dogmatize about the origin of every story that comes to him. He will be content if he can see that the explanation offered is reasonable and if he can determine the general type under which it will fall.

I may sum up my view of Miracles by saying that there is a certain class of details (which I have described in a way that I think will be recognizable, though others may prefer to describe them differently) which I believe will be found in the last resort to belong rather to the story than to the ultimate facts which lie behind the story; and the form which the story takes is determined by the ideas current in the minds of the narrators.

(4) (§§ XVIII–XXVI, pp. 145–67). We have been considering and discussing the permanent and variable elements in the Christian Religion under the heading 'Form and Content in the Christian Tradition'. But we have not yet succeeded in reaching very much common ground. We agree that there is a real distinction between Form and Content; but Mr. Williams seems to me to be inclined to minimize this distinction, and I suppose that in like manner I shall seem to him to magnify it. This holds good especially in regard to what I have called the 'relativity of expression'. Mr. Williams seems to me not to do justice to this, but rather to try to explain it away. He is so anxious to make his forms unchangeable that he prac-

Preface

tically in many cases—and I think I may say in all the disputed cases—confuses form and content altogether.

I should very much like to make one more attempt to expound my views on this subject before I close. All our other differences run up into this.

I sometimes wonder whether it would not be well to revive the use of an old word, in a somewhat different application from that which has been usual—the word 'dispensation'. 'Period' might serve the purpose; but it would bring out only the idea of limitation in time, without that of the orderly and organized arrangement of contents in time. If we look back over the history of human thought from its first dawnings until now, we might say that it has passed through a number of 'dispensations'—such as the prehistoric, the ethnic, that of the Old Testament, that of the New Testament or of Christian Origins, the patristic, the mediaeval or scholastic, the modern. All this time man has been seeking after God, and all this time God has been drawing towards Himself and gradually enlightening the spirit of man. Whatever we are able to describe or reconstruct in imagination of the thought of the past has been the resultant of these two operations—conscious and unconscious effort and aspiration on the part of man and (we may well believe) a gracious leading and assistance on the part of God. Of course there has been no hard-and-fast line between the different dispensations; there have been no abrupt transitions, but each has melted gradually into the next. For purposes of thought they stand out with sufficient clearness; and yet there has been a continuous thread of assisted endeavour running through them. Age is linked to age; and yet, within each age as well as throughout the historic process from first to last, the thought of man has always been a whole. It has never really been so broken up into compartments that any one compartment lost touch and relation with the rest. Rather, there has been a constant interplay ; each side of man's being has worked in with every other. This applies to the highest of his faculties as well as to the lowest ; it applies to his thoughts about God as much as to his other interests in life—such as literature and art and science, industry and commerce, political and social relations. But in any given 'dispensation' man can only use the mental outfit that belongs to him in his place in that dispensation ; his ideas are derived from and proportioned to the particular stage that he has reached in cultural development. His ideas about God are no exception to the rule. In proportion as we conceive of the true infinitude and wonder of the Being of God we shall feel more and more the inadequacy of our petty definitions. All these definitions have in them an element that we must call x. They are always tentative and approximate ; whatever else they may do, we are sure that they will never exhaust the reality.

Because there has been in the course of history one Great Manifestation of Godhead, that does not alter the essential conditions. That Manifestation itself is rather subject to them. From the first moment onwards it had to be described in relative terms. It was not merely that the words were relative, but all the subordinate complexes of ideas were relative. This of necessity brought them into contact with, and in part into limitation by, the other ideas current at the time. As these changed, the whole expression changed ; or at least so much of it changed as belonged to the sphere of what is variable. The x element remains what it is ; but it is always x—something that transcends and eludes and is not co-extensive with the definition.

This, I should contend, is true of all the disputed clauses

Preface   xiii

of the Creed. The Virgin Birth, the physical Resurrection and physical Ascension, are all realistic expressions, adapted to the thought of the time, of ineffable truths which the thought of the time could not express in any other way. To conceive of them realistically was natural and right in the age in which they took shape. Speaking for myself and for those who agree with me, I should say that it was no longer natural and therefore no longer to be enforced as right—to be taken, if we please, as a human symbol for x, but not to be identified in any hard-and-fast manner with it. That is why I deprecate the strong insistence on what Mr. Williams calls 'facts'. If, instead of 'facts', he would speak of 'descriptions of facts', I should have less reason to differ from him. He is working in a right direction when he leaves room for an element of agnosticism. Perhaps a better name than 'agnosticism' would be 'a sense—a devout sense—of mystery'. I can quite believe that Mr. Williams would agree with me in this. For myself, as I have said, I do not deny, and have no wish to deny. I would rather fall back upon the parable : ' the servants say unto him, Wilt thou then that we go and gather them up ? But he saith Nay ; lest haply while ye gather up the tares, ye root up the wheat with them. Let both grow together until the harvest.' I would not even, in this connexion, speak of 'tares'. If I did, it would only be in order to distinguish that which is transitory from that which is eternal. ' When that which is perfect is come, then that which is in part shall be done away.'

I know that I shall be thought of as an innovator, and I know that there are many who—whatever I may do or say—will not forgive me for what I have written in the way of innovation. That cannot be helped. But I hope that they will not go away with an exaggerated idea of the extent to which I am really innovating. *As a spiritual system*, Christianity remains for me just precisely what it has always been. There are not a few Christian beliefs in my interpretation of which I may be held to be behind the times. The Bible is still to me the highest authority that I know. But it is true that I pin my faith not so much to what the Bible says as to what I believe that it means to say ; in other words, not so much to what it said in the letter to those to whom it was first given as to what it says in the spirit to us now. It is in the Bible *considered as history* that the change is greatest. But, even here, I would do no more than put that construction upon it that I should do without hesitation if it had been a less sacred book. Many will think that its sacredness precludes this. But it is just there—and I think, in principle, only there—that I join issue with them.

W. SANDAY.

June 1916.

PS. The reference in the first paragraph of this Preface was to a similar Discussion between the Dean of Christ Church and the writer, which was to have been entitled *Spirit, Matter, and Miracle*, and which it was hoped to publish along with the present volume. It was the continuation of a debate opened by a pamphlet by the Dean, in criticism of one of mine, published in the spring of 1914. The Dean had very kindly agreed that, as in the present case with Mr. Williams, we should each state our case under the same cover. The scheme worked out on similar lines, in three papers on each side ; and the first paper was written in the month of July. Then suddenly came the War, and the Dean, as Vice-Chancellor of the University, was at once involved in a mass of new and very varied and onerous work. Yet in spite of this, the discussion ran its somewhat intermittent course, and some months ago was brought to a conclusion. But on looking back over it we felt that it had lost so much of its original interest, that the controversy out of which it arose had been so far forgotten, and that the public mind was now so deeply occupied with other things, that the best course on the whole was to let our intention lapse and not go on to publication. The same objections did not seem to lie in the same degree to the other debate, which has been spread over a shorter period of time and is more self-contained, the paper out of which it arose being reprinted. It must, however, be confessed that what was begun as a pamphlet has grown practically into a book.

W. S.

ON CONTINUITY OF THOUGHT AND RELATIVITY OF EXPRESSION

THERE is the same problem in the world of thought and in the world of external nature—the problem of reconciling the elements of permanence and stability with the elements of change. Since the days of Heraclitus it has been seen that, from one point of view, all things are in flux : as he penetratingly puts it, ' No man sets foot twice in the same stream.' It is true that in another place he admits that in one sense we may be said to do this, while in another we do not.[1] And our own poet Wordsworth, using the same illustration, draws from it an opposite moral. In one of his Duddon sonnets he rebukes himself for dwelling too much on the transitoriness of life :

> For, backward, Duddon, as I cast my eyes,
> I see what was, and is, and will abide ;
> Still glides the Stream, and shall for ever glide ;
> The Form remains, the Function never dies.

It is true that the stream is flowing and its waters are for no two seconds the same ; even its banks are crumbling, and even in its bed silt is forming and pebbles are rolling down. And yet, on a broader view, the stream continues; it occupies the same place in the landscape, and irrigates the same meadows.

The Form remains, the Function never dies.

It is so with the Christian Faith. There are the great

---

[1] Ritter and Preller, § 26, Plat. *Cratyl.* 402 A:

Λέγει που ‘Ηράκλειτος ὅτι πάντα χωρεῖ καὶ οὐδὲν μένει, καὶ ποταμοῦ ῥοῇ ἀπεικάζων τὰ ὄντα λέγει ὡς δὶς ἐς τὸν αὐτὸν ποταμὸν οὐκ ἂν ἐμβαίης.

The other fragment has :

Ποταμοῖσι τοῖσιν αὐτοῖσιν ἐμβαίνομέν τε καὶ οὐκ ἐμβαίνομεν, εἰμέν τε καὶ οὐκ εἰμεν.

Heraclitus was an astonishing person.

truths about God and Christ ; there are the great broad fundamental experiences of the Christian life. These are permanent and unchangeable. And yet, the forms under which we conceive of them must of necessity change, with the changing apparatus of thought through which they find expression. Every age has its own intellectual outfit. It can but use the tools that it has. When it is using the language of another age, it is like David in Saul's armour ; it loses all its freedom and efficiency of motion.

I

Corresponding to these conditions there are two guiding principles, which really run through all our study of the Christian past, and should never be lost sight of. They are complementary to each other.

On the one hand, there is the *continuity of thought*, in conjunction with the identity of object. All Christian endeavour in all the ages has been concentrated on God and Christ. It has had for its aim to enrich and deepen man's conception of Both (an orthodox thinker would say of the Triune God) as the objects of his worship and devotion.

This identity of object and continuity of aim and effort, worked out in the fellowship of the corporate body through the successive ages of Christian history, has been the element of permanence and the bond and pledge of loyalty.

On the other hand, there is the principle which clearly recognizes throughout this process the persistent *relativity of expression*. This is, in like manner, the guarantee of movement, of progress, of reality and freedom.

This latter principle of the ' relativity of expression ' is as yet by no means fully understood. It is at least far from being consistently grasped and acted upon. Indeed there is one widespread theory which is diametrically opposed to it.

This is the theory according to which the whole body of

Christian doctrine is regarded as an 'unalterable deposit'.[1] But I must speak frankly and say that, for myself, I believe that theory to be, root and branch, from first to last, wholly untenable. It is in direct conflict with the necessity and nature of things, and with most certain facts.

It is commonly based on certain scriptural passages in which the Christian Faith is spoken of as a 'deposit' (παραθήκη, 1 Tim. vi. 20, 2 Tim. i. 12–14), and especially on that phrase in the Epistle of St. Jude (v. 3), 'the faith once delivered unto the saints'. But no one has ever proved, or can prove, that these expressions are a prophetic anticipation of the whole body of Christian tradition, down to and beyond the Athanasian Creed. The Christian faith at the time when the words were written was a very much simpler and less complicated thing. I know it will be said that the later developments were implicitly contained in this earlier nucleus, as the oak is contained in the acorn. But there is just this most important difference that, whereas the original words apply to that which is most permanent in the faith—I do not say that even they are identical with it—the present-day application of them is made to cover all that is most relative in it.

One would have thought that the, perhaps at first sight, somewhat ambiguous language of the Epistles would be

---

[1] Those who are acquainted with Mr. R. A. Knox's little tract, *Modernism: Two Views of the Truth*, will not miss the allusion. As I am referring to this, I should wish to express my sincere gratitude for the kindly words which occur in the course of it, more particularly for the distinction which is drawn between some forms of French Modernism and the English variety of the same opinions. It is quite true that in this controversy, 'both sides believe passionately in the existence of some kind of intellectual duty'. It is also a great pleasure to read the following: 'I do not want here to make any imputations of dishonesty or disingenuity about those who profess their belief in these formulas in a different sense from that which I attach to them myself. I am perfectly confident that their intentions are pure in the sight of God.'

sufficiently guarded from misunderstanding by the Parable of the Talents in the Gospel. The Christian faith is a talent to be traded with and used, and no doubt to be somewhat worn, and even defaced, in using; it was certainly never meant to be wrapped up in a napkin.

But, apart from this, the 'deposit-theory', in the form in which it is employed, is to my mind neither more nor less than a vast *petitio principii*. It is made to include whatever its supporters wish it to include, and to exempt them from the necessity of establishing their case on more rigorous grounds.

I need not say to my present audience how impossible it is to isolate a single department of knowledge, and to regard it as immune from the influence of time and the progress of thought. Those who speak of an 'unalterable deposit', are simply deceiving themselves. There is not, and cannot be, any such thing in the world we live in. I strongly suspect that, even while they use this language, they are exemplifying the fact in their own persons.

We recall to mind those impressive lines of Matthew Arnold's:

> Below the surface stream, shallow and light,
> Of what we *say* we feel—below the stream,
> As light, of what we *think* we feel, there flows
> With noiseless current strong, obscure and deep,
> The central stream of what we feel indeed.[1]

Many people stop short at the surface level. They say their Creeds on what they believe to be sufficient grounds, and honestly think that, with that, their duty is done. For such minds, the questions which others discuss openly and consciously, are relegated to the region of the subconscious. So far as such questions are entertained at all, it is subconsciously and not consciously. The hatches are shut down upon them.

However this may be, there can be no doubt that for

[1] *St. Paul and Protestantism*, p. 83; compare *Life and Letters of Matthew Arnold* ii, 29. I owe this second reference to a friend.

every one, some of the beliefs stored up in his mind are far more living and active than others. The rest he holds in a descending scale of tenacious vitality. Some of them are like atrophied members of the human body; for practical purposes they are quite dead. The reason is that the life-blood no longer flows through them; they are not assimilated; they are so much waste matter. The man *says* that he believes them and *thinks* that he believes them (quite honestly); but he does not believe them indeed. And it is only in its higher sense that I can bring myself to use the word ' belief '.

> One word is too often profaned
> For me to profane it.

Truth is correspondence with reality, or with the best conception we can form of reality. And the test of truth is the extent of this correspondence. Truth imposed, or truth that a man is compelled to *say*, is to me no truth at all.

II

All this that I have been saying seems to me to be no matter of speculation and theory, as to which there can be discussion to decide whether it is right or wrong, but plain statement of fact. It may of course be taken or left; but in my belief it ought to be taken.

Applying it to the history of Christianity, the different phases of Christian doctrine are all so many attempts to express some broad idea in the forms that appealed most to the particular age to which they belonged. This tendency appears from the very first and within the New Testament itself. It could not be otherwise. There can be no doubt that St. Paul's presentation of the doctrine of the Atonement was determined largely by his Pharisaic training. Behind it there lies a deep and intense conviction; but the forms in which that conviction is expressed came from his surroundings. In the age which immediately followed, the metaphor of 'ransom' was most prominent. Anselm elaborated his views in connexion with mediaeval juristic ideas of 'satisfaction'; and so on. In other words, each of these phases in the history of the doctrine was relative to the age through which it was passing, and took its shape from the whole body of thought prevailing at the time. It is easy to prove this, and it has been abundantly proved—last, and not least, in Dr. Rashdall's recent Bampton Lectures. But, that does not the least mean, in my view of the matter, that the doctrine of the Atonement is reduced to nothing and finally disposed of. In all this working of the human mind on the subject of the Atonement, there were elements of permanence as well as elements that were transitory and ephemeral. If we would see what these are, I believe that our best course is to go back behind the Christian era altogether, to Isaiah liii. and the associated passages of the Old Testament. If I understood him rightly, in those of his Lectures which I was able to hear, Dr. Rashdall contented himself with referring to these, and did not expound or apply them. But, from my point of view, this is like putting on the stage the play of *Hamlet* with the part of Hamlet left out.

The doctrine of the Atonement is to my mind a very good example of the necessity for a balanced combination of the principle of continuity of thought with relativity of expression. And I would extend this principle all round. I believe that it holds good equally well in the more audacious departures of the present day.

III

I will take my courage in my hands and speak to you for a moment about one of these audacious departures. I am before you as a suspect, as one under a cloud, because of the opinion which I have expressed on the subject of the Virgin Birth. The opportunity seems to me suitable for saying exactly, or as exactly as I can, what I really think on this subject. I am in a position to do so now rather more maturely than when last I alluded to it.

I should be prepared, if I had the time, to enter into full detail and to examine the evidence on the subject as a whole. But that would be impossible on this occasion, and I do not know when I shall be able to attempt it.

I said some time ago—I do not at the moment remember where, but that does not matter—that I will not put, [or be a party to putting] 'nots' into the Creeds. Some people may think that I have changed my mind; but I have not. I will not affirm everything in the Creeds— but that is different. That is precisely where I draw the line, and believe myself to be right in drawing the line. It is also, if I am not mistaken, where our Bishops drew the line in the joint resolutions which they issued last year. I believe that they exercised a very wise discretion. I speak for myself, and for my own confession of faith. I do not doubt that there are some who will say that, having gone so far, I ought to go the next step further; and some might hint that I drew back to save my skin. So far as I know myself and my own motives, it is not to save my skin. If I thought it the honest thing to say a point-blank No, I do not think that I should hesitate to say it. But I plead guilty to being one of those who believe that truth lies in a *nuance*; and this—the difference between not affirming and denying—is the precise *nuance* in which I think it lies. The abstinence from (full) affirmation is consistent with a great amount of partial affirmation.

I will explain just what I believe to have been, and in a manner to be, the real function of the clause in the Creed about the Virgin Birth.

The Jews, as we know, used habitually to speak of raising 'a fence or hedge round the Law'. We should perhaps more naturally take a metaphor from fortification, and speak of 'throwing up an outwork' in front of our citadel. In either case the idea would be of keeping the enemy at arm's length; putting an additional obstacle in his way, before he could begin to lay sap or mine to the keep or centre of the position. If one may venture to ascribe motives to the Almighty, that is why I believe Him to have decreed that the full belief in the Virgin Birth should prevail for so long. There are abundant analogies for this in the authenticated history of mankind and, more particularly, in the history of the reception and interpretation of the Creeds. One of the greatest mistakes which men have made, and are still making, about God, is in attributing to Him, in the ages of the past as well as in the present, what I may venture to call a punctilious determination of the will towards securing the prevalence throughout the world of what we call 'literal' truth. All through the early ages of mankind 'poetical' truth has been the rule, and 'literal' the exception. This may be different from what we should expect. But anyhow it is plain matter of fact, and we must not shut our eyes to it. It is not for us to know the reasons for this particular characteristic of the workings of Divine Providence; they are beyond us, and belong to those vast rangings through time and space by which these workings are governed. It may well be that 'the times of this ignorance', or of this latitude, are coming to an end. We are not concerned with the future, but only with the past; and in regard to the past we must resign ourselves not to know, or to know very imperfectly. Even we men, dull-sighted and fallible as we are, can see a multitude of reasons, short of its literal truth, for the prevalence of the belief in the Virgin Birth; it has been of immense and prolonged benefit to mankind. Even at this day, it goes hard to let it drop out of our range of vision; and only (what some of us think) imperious necessity compels us to loosen our hold upon it. I should on all grounds, and in particular out of piety towards the past, refuse to deny the Virgin Birth. Those who will may think that I am splitting a hair in doing so. But I find myself able to *subsume the idea of the Virgin Birth under the yet larger and more important idea of Supernatural Birth*. I will venture to express my meaning in a phrase : it all seems to me to stand (*sit venia verbo*) *for the direct influx of Deity into manhood*.

We are prepared for such a conception by our belief in Divine Immanence ; it is no strain upon us to conceive of a supreme and unique act and form of this Immanence. And, with all possible deference for my revered friend, Dr. Swete, if we can conceive of it under a form that is in accordance with nature, that is far easier for some of us than to think of it under conditions that we should call *contra naturam*.

Again, if I had time, I should be prepared to show that this form of the conception was entirely congruous with all the Old Testament analogies. The Jews—without any exception, so far as I know—thought of divine intervention in human births as something *superadded* to the natural process, not as a mutilation of it. The idea of divine fatherhood taking the place of human fatherhood, is pagan and not Jewish. That is one of the puzzles attaching to the stories of the Nativity in St. Matthew and St. Luke. I am not sure that anything un-Jewish is implied by the latter Evangelist. It is implied—or shall I say, half-implied ?—by the former ; for there are traces, not wholly obliterated, that the Genealogy which he incorporated, originally ended ' Joseph begat Jesus '. I doubt if the other idea arose actually in Palestine ; I suspect that it came in somewhere on the outskirts, from Syrian syncretism.

IV

We are met for counsel, and I would venture to expand the main point of what I have just been saying into a piece of more general advice or suggestion. I think that we should all be on our guard against 'denials'.

10 *Form and Content in Christian Tradition*

I do not think that a blank and unqualified denial—putting a 'not' into the Creed—is anywhere required of us.

Incidentally I may observe—not as a motive, but as a simple statement of fact—that by abstaining from denials we make our own position as English Churchmen impregnable. So long as we are on our guard against the point-blank 'not', no one can touch us.

This may be worldly wisdom, but, to my thinking, it is truth as well. And it is because it is truth that I commend the advice to you.

Relative truth, it should be remembered, is still essentially truth and not falsehood. For many long centuries it may have been the best truth available. In any case, it is what God has willed for a time, if not in permanence; and we can never think or speak of it otherwise. That fact alone precludes the possibility of 'denial'. Relative truth is not negatived but superseded. The nearest analogy in nature is the way in which the snake sloughs its skin. The old skin does not come off until the new skin is fully formed.

V

There is another practical suggestion which I will make, if you will allow me. Our object is to keep up the fullest possible continuity with the past. Whatever the outside world may think of us, we are not disloyal; we are not indifferent to our inheritance. We too are anxious that 'all our days'—all the days of the Christian Church—

> should be
> Bound each to each by natural piety.

Those of us who are students seek to attain this end by an ever deepened study of the past. They undertake that study in no cold, detached, dispassionate spirit. They 'think upon the stones of Zion' as rich with history, as the member of an ancient and illustrious family thinks upon the stones of his ancestral home.

Study undertaken in this spirit cannot be too sympathetic. The mind that has a true sense of continuity will always be seeking—not only to understand the formulae which it is investigating, not only to enter, and to enter fully, into the grounds on which they were based, but to steep itself in the spirit which lay behind them; it will be always trying to catch something of the balance and breadth of view which is distinctive of the decisions of the Church Universal and which marks them off from the narrower shibboleths of the sects. Because we in these latter days are not able to adopt as our own the exact expressions—*iurare in verba*—of the Old Masters, it by no means follows that we shall not have a great reverence for them; that we shall not try to live again their life, and to make the spirit, if not the letter, of their reasoning a pattern for our own.

But the particular point of practical suggestion that I would ask leave to make, is that we should not mix up our study of the past with our attempts at definition and formulation in the present. Ancient and modern are better kept apart. We shall spoil our study of the ancient if we are constantly intruding into it modern questions and modern difficulties; and we shall equally hamper the free endeavour to express ourselves in the language of our own day, if we burden ourselves with questions which really belong to the older context and not to our own. Let us look at the ancient world with the eyes of the ancient world, and then at the modern with the eyes of the modern. Let us try to think out each set of conclusions by itself before we attempt to combine them. When we know accurately what the ancients thought and why they thought it, we shall be better able to find equivalents for their teaching in terms that are frankly and genuinely modern.

VI

It is a great mistake to suppose that we have any desire 'to jettison the Creeds'. I do not say that we might not like if we could—though of course we cannot—to redraft them. Any such idea can at present be nothing more than a pious aspiration. And yet it is, I hope and believe, an aspiration with some substance in it. It may be realized in that day—which our grandchildren may see, if not our children—'the Parliament of Man, the Federation of the World', when the Churches are reunited.

We can conceive even now the lines on which we should like to see the Creeds redrafted. We should like to see them no longer what they largely are—so many negations of heresy, but real constructive summaries of the faith that is in us. In the meantime we look up to them as great historic monuments, landmarks and beacons, which still show us the way we should go, although they are somewhat worn and weather-beaten. We always think of them as what God has willed. They are clothed in language that was natural and suitable at the time—and not only so, but the product of deep and strenuous thinking. Even if we regard them as relative rather than absolute, yet as relative they have the strongest claims on our respectful attention. They are a constant reminder of the direction in which we should aim.

VII

The chief characteristic of our modern thinking about the deepest things in the universe, is its greater *simplicity*. The difference between ancient and modern methods all points in this direction. We should never think now of working out our beliefs with the minuteness aimed at in the Early Creeds. The methods employed in their construction lent themselves to minute definition. They were more like the codifying of a body of law than a statement of the foundations of true religion.

In drawing up the Creeds, the ancients went upon a number of assumptions that we can make no longer. They assumed the strict inerrancy of all the Scriptures; they assumed the literal and equal accuracy of all the narratives of the Old and New Testaments alike. They had behind them a different *Weltanschauung* from ours. They thought of the sky as a solid vault resting on pillars; they thought of the sun and moon and planets as fixed in concentric spheres, which revolved within one another. They believed that irregularities occurred in the order of nature without any of the limitations that we should set to them now. It is really out of the question that the young men of the present day should be expected to subscribe to every item in formulae constructed under conditions such as these.

The principle which enables our young men to accept the Creeds, is that which I have had in view throughout this paper, the principle of the *relativity of expression*. They believe that the Creeds are true, not so much in the minute technical detail which was in men's minds at the time when they were composed, as on broad spiritual lines. They would not deny the technical details; they believe that they all had a certain relative rightness in the periods that understood and could assimilate them; they are perfectly ready to believe that the good Providence of God presided over the whole evolution. But they, none the less, believe that God has ' provided some better thing for us, that they, without us, should not be made perfect '.

It does not really matter that all the living beliefs of the present day cannot be put, or must be imperfectly put, into words. A great deal may remain as a matter of feeling rather than of words; in the sense in which Wordsworth wrote :

We feel that we are greater than we know.

The central belief of Christendom is itself an example of this. All the terms in which it is described in the New

Testament are themselves relative terms. They all have their history, and they must be interpreted in accordance with that history. Of course we must fill our minds with this to the very best of our ability. It may not, in the end, be easy to digest the result into a sentence. But we shall most certainly go away saying to ourselves, ' My Lord and my God.'

VIII

If the main result of modern thought as applied to the subject-matter of the Creeds is a general tendency towards simplification, that should remove from those who are committed to it at least one of the accusations that are often brought against them. We are told that Modernism tends to place a gap between the learned and the simple. Just the contrary. It tends to bring the learned and the simple nearer together. Its whole effect ought to be to induce the learned to formulate their beliefs in terms which they can share whole-heartedly with the simple. It is really the Traditionalists who do what they accuse us of doing. They would bind upon the unlearned all the technical apparatus of ancient tradition. Of course they bind it upon themselves as well as upon others. But, to say the truth, they do not succeed in binding it upon either. The human spirit refuses to be bound in such a way. As a matter of fact, they exemplify those lines of Matthew Arnold's. They know what they *say* they feel, and they know what they *think* they feel; but they do not know what they feel indeed.

What does the average worshipper really make of the Nicene and Athanasian Creeds ? What does he really make of many of the Psalms and Lessons ? There is always enough left of which he can make something, but in these parts of the services there must be always a great deal that is simply unassimilated.

So far from setting a premium upon learning, the tendency of the modernist is all the other way. He regards the Creeds as products of excessive intellectualism. What he wants to do is to get out of the grooves of these over-minute and sometimes superfluous definitions. The modernist seeks for his ideal quite at the other end of the scale. He is moved to his depths by the sight of the simple saint upon his knees. He would like to put into his creed,

> Except ye be converted, and become as little children, ye shall in no wise enter into the kingdom of heaven.

All this does not prevent the man to whom is committed the talent of learning from making such use of it as he can. It is part of the obligation laid upon him. But he would, none the less, join from his heart in St. Paul's correction,

> And yet show I unto you a more excellent way.

IX

One other consequence follows from this. The genuine modernist, who has really taken in the principle of 'the relativity of expression', will have no false pedantry about him in disparaging the value of either the thought or the expression of previous ages. If he seeks to express his own thought in the sincerest language he can find, it is not from any petty ambition to be 'up to date'. He has no Pharisaical feeling of superiority towards his next door neighbour who remains at a less advanced stage. He is concerned with his own duty, and he avoids comparisons of this kind. He always respects the honest convictions of another, even though they may be a little behind the times. It is better to be behind the times than to be puffed up with the conceit of theories half digested and half understood. It is always safe advice to one who is struggling out of one phase into another, not to be in too great a hurry but to make sure of his ground, to proceed *pedetentim*, by one step at a time.

X

The great aim (as I have said in another place) of the Modernist Quest is *the unification of thought*. There have been times when the thought of an age has been completely unified. It was so in Clement of Alexandria and Origen ; it was so in St. Thomas Aquinas and the Schoolmen. But from the Reformation onwards, with the insistence upon verbal inspiration on the one side, and with the development of the natural sciences and of a purely lay philosophy on the other, there was for a long time an increasing divergence between theology and secular thinking. This began to be reduced as the critical movement gradually made itself felt ; and various half measures have been taken, and various half-way halting-places have been erected. But only with the rise of Modernism can it be said that the frank and full unification of secular and religious thought has come to be faced as a definite ideal. We may be sure that, once clearly grasped, this ideal will not be let go again.

Until the beginning of Modernism, the Church of Christ had been content to let unification go by the board. There has always been one little corner of the globe that has been exempted from the rules, a *hortus inclusus* to which the methods and hypotheses applicable elsewhere were held not to apply. We desire to make the methods that we apply to it strictly homogeneous. We are convinced that life in New Testament times was not conducted as if in the atmosphere of a dark séance. We are convinced that bodies in those days did not float in the air or materialize and dematerialize at will. We have no doubt in our own minds that, of the two hypotheses—that these things really happened, and that they came to be thought to have happened on the basis of widely prevalent ideas— the latter is by far the more probable. The belief in this enables us to throw open the doors of the dark chamber, and to let in light and air.

When Mr. Knox, in his easy-going manner, paraphrases or parodies our view of the *Descensus ad Inferos* as meaning that

> Since the people of the time [of Christ] were the sort of people they were, that is just the sort of thing they would have thought He did,

he is saying exactly what we really think; and we have practically no doubt that the explanation is the most probable that can be given. And I am afraid I must reply to another critic of mine that it is not a tenable view to apply this kind of explanation to the *Descensus* and to refuse to apply it to other clauses of the Creed.

I know that it will seem an audacious, and even a presumptuous thing to say, but I am almost as sure as I am of anything that the view which I have just been propounding can be permanently maintained, and I greatly doubt whether any other view can.

For myself, I have always said that I do not deny the reality of miracle. What I contend for is that there are in the nature of things (i. e. in the world as God has made it) limitations to miracle of which the men of our Lord's day were not aware, but of which we are aware now.

I must confess that, since the War began, it has absorbed all my thoughts, and I am behindhand with my theological reading. I have not yet read either Dr. Headlam's book or Dr. Illingworth's. I know that, when I do read them, it will be with all respect. The writers are sure to have stated with the greatest ability the view opposed to mine. But I cannot think that they are likely to lead me to change an opinion which it has taken me a lifetime to form.

XI

I might stop here. But I am tempted to send out this paper with an Envoi of a more personal kind. It has been inevitable that I should take the line I have done, and at this time of day it is not likely—indeed I may say it is impossible—that I should change it. I know that, in consequence, many of my old friends look askance at me. It is the sorrow of my declining years. It cannot be helped, and I do not wish to complain. They think that I have ceased to be true to the cause that I have had at heart ever since I began to write. They are too kind and too gentle to say this in words. They leave that to those who do not know me.

There is nothing of which I wish to complain. But I cannot help thinking that even my friends have shown a certain slowness of understanding. The fault is very probably mine. The present is indeed the first time that I have succeeded (if I have succeeded) in stating my more recent views as a connected whole. I know that the statement is of the most summary kind; but they are words addressed to the wise, which wise men (if they care to do so) can easily fill in for themselves. What I have said may at least help to dissipate some of the ideas that are still entertained about me. Those who are a little further removed credit me with a number of presuppositions which I should utterly repudiate. They think that I take a mechanical view of the universe, and nothing could be further from my mind. But there are two things that even some of my nearest friends seem to me to have been slow in seeing. They do not see that I myself regard my own position within the Church of England as absolutely loyal and absolutely inexpugnable. The force of association is exceedingly strong, and it is difficult to place oneself in the attitude of another whose premisses are different. I know that I am running up against the prejudices (as I must needs call them, for they are not reasoned processes), not only of the Traditionalist, but of the plain man. If I cannot rest in either of these two positions, the reason is that both seem to me untenable. But I wonder if this paper will succeed in making my friends see things more as I do.

And then, secondly, I do not think that they at all

appreciate the enormous strength of the position I am defending, or the hope it holds out of winning thinking men in the modern world to Christ. I cannot see that any of them have allowed due weight to what I have called ' the unification of thought '. The mind that has no vision of this cannot do justice to the mind that is guided by it. If we can bring Christianity into a system of unified thought, I do not see what should prevent the whole world from becoming Christian.

I must admit that what I have written has a double edge to it. It is meant, primarily, for the Churchmen's Union. But it is meant, hardly less, for my own friends who do not go with me. It is meant as an invitation to Christians to make common cause all round. If my position is really as sound, from the point of view of orthodox criticism, as I believe it to be, there ought to be no impediment to our working together. If I am not unorthodox—and I claim distinctly that I am not ; I claim that I am only re-interpreting the Creeds, as they must inevitably be re-interpreted ; if that is so, traditional Churchmen should be able to work with me ; and, if with me (perhaps with some little adjustment and explanation) with the members of the Churchmen's Union as well. It is hardly right for me to speak for them, as I am not a member of the body, though in sympathy with it. But I have little real doubt that the Churchmen's Union would welcome the full co-operation of traditional Christians. They would welcome it for their own sakes. They would be glad to think that the Church of Christ has a Liberal wing and a Conservative wing, and that each is necessary to the other. They would rejoice to feel that the Conservative wing was there, to state always the Conservative side of each question as it came up as forcibly as possible. As Liberals, they would like to have some guarantee that the other side did not go by default. There are men on the other side for whom I (for one) have the profoundest respect. If they think I am wrong, I wish they would try to convert me. But, if they do, they must show a better understanding of my premisses than they have allowed to appear hitherto. I would not ask them to change their own views, although I believe them to be untenable. But I would ask them to face the problem whether, even from their own presuppositions, we cannot all work together. If they can answer that question in the affirmative, I see no reason why there should not really be one flock and one Shepherd.

MR. N. P. WILLIAMS'S FIRST LETTER

My dear Dr. Sanday,—

I am venturing to send you herewith a few notes on your paper 'Continuity of Thought and Relativity of Expression'. My excuse for so doing is the fact that in the paper you express the wish that 'those on the other side' would try to 'convert' you. I am very far from claiming competence for such a task, which, I imagine, would require both learning and mental powers no less than your own: but I can at least suggest the line which 'the other side' would be inclined to take as against some of your contentions: and exchange of ideas between the two 'sides' can in any case do no harm.

I may, perhaps, say to begin with that I do not propose to deal at all with one question which occupies a certain amount of space in your paper—and that is the question of 'loyalty' to the Church of England. As things are, I have not the slightest desire to question the (subjective) *bona fides* of any one who feels that he can conscientiously belong to that Church. And, in any case, the 'Church of England' aspect of the question is clearly of subordinate importance, compared to the main issue as to what is *true*. I shall therefore endeavour to discuss the question on its merits, without any reference to the particular conditions of Anglicanism. The word 'Church' will occur occasionally towards the end of my remarks, but this will always mean the Church Catholic.

For the sake of clearness, I have ventured to cast these notes into something like the shape of a review, which I now subjoin.

I

After some general remarks on the philosophic problem of identity and change, you begin by positing two principles the recognition of which should govern all study of the Christian past, namely, (*a*) the *continuity of Christian thought*, in conjunction with the identity of its object, that is, God revealed in Christ, and (*b*) the *relativity of its expression*. I have no fault to find with this setting out of the subject for debate, and (in senses which I hope to explain presently) I should be prepared to accept both these principles. Perhaps I may be able to develop the criticisms, which I shall venture to make upon your presentation of them, with the greatest clearness, if I begin at once from the first point at which I find myself in disagreement with your paper, that is, your denial that the Christian Faith may rightfully be spoken of as an ' unalterable deposit ' (p. 3).

II

I cannot help thinking that on this point you and Knox (or at any rate you and—shall I say myself ?) are rather at cross-purposes. The reasonable Traditionalist (I should say) is very far from claiming that our Lord dictated the Nicene or Athanasian Creeds verbally as they stand to the disciples during the Great Forty Days, or that the precise and elaborate definitions of the fifth century were explicitly present to the minds of primitive Christians in the first. All that he maintains is that Christianity is not a mere mode of feeling, but includes as one of its constituent elements a definite body of *ideas* : that these ideas have been revealed by God through Jesus Christ, not merely excogitated by man from his own inner consciousness : that the task of conserving these ideas has been committed to the Christian Church ; and that it is not competent for the Church to alter, suppress, or mutilate these ideas in their essential nature, inasmuch as they come to us on divine authority (though there is no reason why the Church should not utilize all the conceptual instruments employed by the thought of each age as it passes in order to the better and clearer formulation of these ideas). But all this (I imagine, though I refrain from speaking categorically) does not go beyond what you say or imply in your remarks on the first of your two principles, that of the continuity of thought. I gather that you would not deny that a Revelation did happen in the first century of our era, and that there is such a thing as a body of Christian ideas which it is our duty to hand on to succeeding generations unimpaired. Of course, we might differ as to what ideas really do belong to the essential body of Christian truth and what not : but that there *is* such a body (I imagine) we should be both agreed. When Catholic theologians (at any rate those of modern times and modern sympathies) speak of the ' deposit of Faith ' as unalterable, I take them to mean unalterable *in its essential content* (as, indeed, it must be if it really is a divine message) rather than in its verbal, or even in its conceptual form. Certainly I should not maintain the ' unalterableness ' of the deposit in any sense which would exclude Development as explained by Newman in his Essay on the Development of Doctrine. On our view, it is only of the *essential content* that ' unalterableness ' can be predicated *simpliciter*, not of the verbal form in which it is enshrined or the categories used to envisage it. I do not deny that we should also predicate ' unalterableness ' in a sense, and *secundum quid*, of the forms—but I will discuss that presently.

As an instance of such an ' unalterable ' idea I would suggest the general conception of Jesus Christ as Son of God, in a sense in which no other man has been or can be, by direct Filiation and not by Adoption, pre-existing eternally in the bosom of the Father before His human birth. Or, again, there is the idea of the Atonement, which you yourself instance on p. 5 f. I am surely not wrong in supposing that you would regard these two ideas as being elements in a permanent trust committed to the Christian Church, which, however much they may be explained or elucidated, no succeeding generation would be at liberty to explain away or to abolish.

It would clear the ground, therefore, if we could agree upon the following propositions :

    I. In the Christian Faith as it has come down to us we can distinguish between *form* and essential *content*.

    II. The essential *content* (at least) is beyond the power of man to alter, whatever may be said about the *form* or *expression*.

But I need not labour the point further, because you say yourself on p. 1 f. : ' There are the great truths about God and Christ : there are the great broad fundamental experiences of the Christian life. *These are permanent and unchangeable*' (italics mine). This gives me all I want at this stage of the argument. I hope that I am not taking too optimistic a view of your remarks on the ' continuity of thought ', in suggesting that the differences which separate you from reasonable Traditionalists are on this precise point differences of terminology rather than of conception : but when I read passages like that on p. 10 f. :

> Whatever the outside world may think of us, we are not disloyal ; we are not indifferent to our inheritance. We too are anxious that ' all our days '—all the days of the Christian Church—
>
>   ' should be
> Bound each to each by natural piety.'
>
> Those of us who are students seek to attain this end by an ever-deepened study of the past. They undertake that study in no cold, detached, dispassionate spirit. They ' think upon the stones of Zion ' as rich with history, as the member of an ancient and illustrious family thinks upon the stones of his ancestral home.
>
> Study undertaken in this spirit cannot be too sympathetic. The mind that has a true sense of continuity will always be seeking—not only to understand the formulae which it is investigating, not only to enter, and to enter fully, into the grounds on which they were based, but to steep itself in the spirit which lay behind them ; it will be always trying to catch something of

the balance and breadth of view which is distinctive of the decisions of the Church Universal and which marks them off from the narrower shibboleths of the sects.

—couched in language of affecting beauty, which chimes in exactly with my own thoughts and emotions on these points, I am emboldened to hope that here, at least, the difference is not one of vital principle.

III

I now come to a more difficult and contentious question, that of the principle of *relativity of expression*. For the sake of clearness, I will endeavour to formulate what I conceive to be the gist of your argument in compendious shape, so as to be able to put my finger upon the exact point where we begin to diverge. If I am not mistaken, it can be thrown into the form of three propositions and a conclusion, viz.

1. At the beginning of Christianity, its essential ideas were much more vague, fluid, and undefined in outline than now.
2. In the course of centuries, certain technical forms were imposed upon these originally rather vague ideas. As the result of reflection and discussion, they became hardened into *theologumena*, sharply-defined concepts, and woven together into an elaborate and interconnected system—that of ecclesiastical and conciliar ' Orthodoxy '.
3. The ancient theologians, upon whom was laid the task of fixing and defining the essential ideas of Christianity, had to do the work with the best tools and in the best environment and atmosphere at their disposal. But
    (a) the philosophical categories and modes of thought, with which their minds were furnished, were peculiar to the ancient world, and have been long since outgrown by modern thought,

And

(b) the Fathers, in their reflection upon the great ideas of Christianity, started from an assumption which we now know to be erroneous, viz. that of the verbal inerrancy of the Scriptures.

And

(c) the ordered knowledge of the facts of the physical world, which we call natural science, was practically a sealed book to them (p. 13, ll. 1–15).

CONCLUSION. Inasmuch, therefore, as the ancients worked with tools and in an atmosphere which would not be satisfactory to the modern mind, their results must be expected *a priori* to be tainted with the same unsatisfactoriness. ' It is really out of the question that the young men of the present day should be expected to subscribe to every item in formulae constructed under conditions such as these ' (p. 13, ll. 12–15). Consequently, the detailed language of the Creeds and Ecumenical Definitions may be said to be true, or to have been true, relatively to the world of knowledge in which, and the thought-forms with which the ancients worked : but, relatively to the world of modern knowledge, we can be certain, even before having examined them, that they will prove to be inadequate, and *pro tanto* untrue. Untrue, that is, or only relatively true, in respect of their detailed affirmations, or of some of them : though they may still be said to be broadly true, in the sense that they are fairly successful attempts, by persons who have considerable claims upon our veneration, to formulate true ideas (p. 11, ll. 12–18).

I hope that the above is not an unfair summary of the argument contained expressly or by implication in your paper. It will now be easy for me to indicate the exact points where I must part company with you.

Before, however, proceeding to do this, I should like to note the fact that this argument is all of a purely *a priori* or deductive nature. You do not, apparently, approach the Creeds *a posteriori*, and say ' Behold, this, and this, and this article of the Creeds have been shown by scientific observation or historical research to be as a matter of fact wrong ' ; you seem to say ' Things being what they are, the Creeds must in the nature of the case be expected to be wrong.' I do not complain of this ; the orthodox theologian is the last person in the world to object to the use of the deductive method in theology ; but it is interesting to have it (apparently) admitted that the Modernist campaign against the literal acceptation of the Creeds is based, not so much upon ascertained facts, as upon considerations of *a priori* probability.

However, I must not delay my examination of the argument itself.

I do not wish to challenge Propositions 1 and 2, which seem to me to correspond to facts.

Nor do I dispute the truth of the statements (*b*) and (*c*) (referring to the Fathers' belief in ' verbal inspiration ' and their ignorance of physical science) in Proposition 3.

BUT,

A. I should strenuously deny 3 (*a*)—viz. the statement that the categories used by the Councils in formulating the great ideas of the Faith were such as have been outgrown by the modern world,

AND,

B. Even if Propositions 1, 2, and 3 were all true as they stand, I should still deny that the Conclusion necessarily followed from them.

I append a few remarks upon each of these positions.

28 *Form and Content in Christian Tradition*

IV

With regard to Position A. To say all that there is to be said on this point would require the dimensions of an encyclopaedia, and I must perforce content myself with a few very summary observations. It is commonly asserted by Modernists that the categories and concepts employed by the Fathers and the Councils in the work of defining Orthodoxy are of bewildering complexity and subtleness: that (to use your own words on p. 12), ' the early Creeds ' aimed at working out Christian belief with far more ' minuteness ' than we should now dream of: that the acceptance of Catholic Orthodoxy involves binding upon oneself a vast technical apparatus. I must beg leave to dispute this entirely. The thought-forms of which the Creeds and conciliar Definitions make use seem to me to be quite reasonably few and simple—οὐσία, φύσις, ὑπόστασις, πρόσωπον, θέλημα, ἐνέργεια, and the like. Personally I do not see how the Fathers, or anybody else, could have got on with less, if they were going to define anything at all. Moreover, I should maintain (these are summary observations) that the categories mentioned above are not peculiar to ancient thought, but are inherent in the structure of human thought as such. In my opinion, they are neither Platonic nor Aristotelian, neither Stoic nor Cynic, but merely common-sense categories. Has any modern logician really produced a better form of thought than the copula, or a more helpful category than that of Substance and Attribute (to which most of the terms used in the controversies of the fourth, fifth, and sixth centuries are really reducible)? I know, of course, that some Liberal historians of dogma accuse the Substance-Attribute category of being ' mechanical ', ' materialistic ', ' non-ethical ', and ' sub-personal '; but, again, I must say that these adjectives seem to me to be mere question-begging epithets, and to be entirely destitute of any logical weight. I am just as entitled to call it 'supra-personal' in order to extol it, as the Liberal has to call it 'sub-personal' in order to depreciate it. I dare say that from the point of view of a disciple of Bergson or Bradley the category of Substance has not much to be said for it—no more, from these same view-points, has the idea of a personal God. yet you at least would hardly describe the idea of a personal God as a worn-out category peculiar to ancient thought. To sum up, it seems to me that the forms of thought employed in the Creeds and Definitions, although abstruse, as the height of the subject demands, are yet simple, clear, and such as will remain valid for the normal human mind until the end of time. I have never found any difficulty in explaining the Chalcedonian doctrine of our Lord's Two Natures to pupils or simple-minded parishioners. I will admit that *if* the Fathers had embodied in the structure of the Creeds such conceptions as Plato's Idea of the Good or Aristotle's πρῶτον κινοῦν ἀκίνητον the reproach of containing outworn forms of thought might justly have been brought against those formularies. but they didn't : and the fact that they didn't, when they might easily have done so, contains to my mind the strongest suggestion that their reflections and decisions were controlled and guided by the heavenly assistance of the Holy Spirit.

V

With regard to Position B (the non-cogency of the Conclusion), the whole argument, as I have ventured to formulate it, seems to be substantially identical with what you call the 'argument from the difference of times' in your pamphlet *Bishop Gore's Challenge to Criticism*: and (if I remember rightly—I am quoting from memory) you observed (*in loc.*), 'Creeds constructed by ancient thinkers cannot, in the nature of things, correspond to the modern mind and its requirements.' (I fear that I have not got the words right, but it was something like that.) I must confess that when I read these words I mentally pronounced the ' argument from the difference of times ' to be a pure *non sequitur*. It seemed to me that you might as well say, Because the men of the fifth century believed twice two to be four, the modern mind must necessarily take it to be five ; or that you would be equally justified in pronouncing the Law of Gravitation to be inexact or unsatisfactory because Newton knew nothing of motor-cars or post-impressionism. Perhaps it is unfair to comment in this way on an argument expressed so summarily. But, even as set out in more detailed shape in your paper, it seems to me to fall considerably short of formal cogency—and that for the following reasons.

In the first place, it leaves out of count the fact *that it is possible to arrive at true conclusions from false, or partially false premisses.*

It is doubtless true, as I have admitted above, that most of the ancients (not all : Clement and Origen and their school, if I mistake not, are exceptions) believed in the verbal inerrancy of the Bible : but that does not prove that their speculations, though based upon erroneous premisses, were not overruled by Divine Providence so as to result in true conclusions. (This is of course what the reasonable Traditionalist would say happened in the case of St. Athanasius and Proverbs viii.)

Moreover, I cannot admit that the ignorance of the ancients in the sphere of physical science necessarily discounts the conclusions at which the Catholic Church arrived in the sphere of religious ideas. Even if we regard the Creeds and conciliar Definitions as merely the products of unassisted human brains, we have no right to assume that ignorance or error in one department of knowledge necessarily involves error in all other departments. This holds good within the sphere of natural science itself : there have been many pioneers in one branch, who have been privileged to throw light upon many dark corners of the universe, but yet have held totally erroneous and fantastic views in regard to other branches of knowledge. And I should also distinguish sharply, for these purposes, between *dogmatic theology*, on the one side, dealing with the contents of the specific Christian revelation, and the *Philosophy of Religion*, on the other, containing the speculations of unassisted human reason on the data of the religious consciousness in general. I dare say that the modern theologian, in so far as he has access to the vast treasuries of observations and generalizations accumulated by modern Natural Science, is infinitely better equipped for conducting the inquiries proper to the Philosophy of Religion, than were the ancients : but I should strongly dispute the suggestion that he is in a better position than they were for formulating the essential contents of the Christian deposit. If one is discussing the mysteries of the Trinity or of the Incarnation, it seems to me that it does not much matter whether the universe is thought to be heliocentric or geocentric. If it be admitted that God created heaven and earth, it matters little whether the distance between the earth and the stars be reckoned in hundreds or in trillions of miles. I wish to speak with perfect openness, and therefore, at the risk of somewhat weakening my argument on this point, I will admit that there is one area in which the spheres of dogma and of natural science do seem to overlap, and in which erroneous conceptions of scientific fact might vitiate and disturb trains of theological reasoning : and that is the subject of the Fall and of Original Sin. *A priori*, I will concede that the Fathers (and, of course, the New Testament writers no less) might well have been seriously handicapped by their ignorance of anthropology and biology in thinking out and clearing up these presuppositions of Christian soteriology. But, even in this particular area, it seems to me that you are not entitled to claim more than a general *a priori* probability (*not* mathematical certainty) for the supposition that the early Church went totally or partially wrong : you must always leave open the possibility that it may have come to true conclusions from erroneous premises.[1]

'Yes,' you may reply, ' but that is all that is claimed— the general *a priori* probability that the conclusions of the early Church were to a certain extent vitiated by the erroneous character of some of its premises. If we know that a thinker has started from false premises, it is surely probable, even though it may not be rigorously certain, that his conclusions are at least unreliable.' I might object that certain phrases and turns of expression ('It is really out of the question . . .' and so on) appear to claim much more than general probability, little less in fact than dogmatic certainty, for your conclusions. But let that pass. I think that I should not be inclined to challenge the last remark which I have ventured hypothetically to attribute to you—viz. the proposition that the Creeds and Ecumenical Definitions are *probably* inaccurate or unsatisfactory—but for one great assumption, which I have kept in the background until now, but which seems to me to be the master-key to the whole controversy.

VI

This great assumption is the belief in *the immanent personal presence of God the Holy Ghost in the Catholic Church*, working in and through the processes of its life, overruling the turbulence and ambition of its leaders, sifting out the categories which are of permanent value and belong to the essential structure of human thought, from the *detritus* of merely temporary and local thought-forms, and inspiring the whole *nexus* of dogmatic development so intimately and pervasively that each doctrine, as it took shape, assumed precisely that *form* which the Holy Spirit foresaw would most perfectly preserve the essential *content* till the end of time. I would suggest

[1] Which, again, is what I believe happened.

that, for those who are able to make this assumption, the 'argument from the assistance of the Holy Spirit' more than cancels any slight weight which I have allowed to the 'argument from the difference of times'. Of course, all language about God and divine things is relative to human conditions of thought : but the point is, that if we can make this assumption of a Real Presence of the Spirit in the Church, we shall be able to feel confidence that the terms which the Councils, under His inspiration, adopted, are, although relative, relative to human thought *überhaupt*—not to any one temporary or local phase of it : in other words, that they not merely *were* the best terms for the Graeco-Roman world of the fifth century, but that they *are* the best terms which are ever likely to be hit upon by human beings.

It will now be clear in what sense I should speak of the verbal and conceptual forms, in which the authority of the Church has enshrined the essential ideas of Christianity, as 'unalterable'. I do not assert that they are 'unalterable' in the sense of having always been there : but I should say that, now that they *are* there, they are unalterable *for the future*. This 'unalterability' has, on our view, two consequences. It means, first, that it is not permissible to substitute other intellectual forms (the *verbal* expression is after all a secondary matter) for those which the Holy Spirit has once sanctioned, speaking through His organ, the Church Universal : and it means, secondly, that it is not permissible to discard these forms in favour of a mere formless vagueness—to reject the clear and precise apprehension of truth which God has given us through His Spirit in the Church, and to relapse into the original indefiniteness on the plea of returning more nearly to the conditions of early Christianity or the intentions of its Founder. These consequences may not be welcome to the modern mind, but it cannot be denied that they follow irresistibly from the assumption of that peculiarly intense and vital presence of the Spirit in the

Church which I have tried to describe above. I am afraid that you may still pronounce the idea of a set of unalterable forms, even understood in this sense, to be *a priori* impossible ('contrary to the nature and necessity of things'); but I would, with all respect, ask you to consider whether the law of universal flux, which you appear to postulate, applies to such things as the multiplication table, the laws of thought, or the axioms of geometry: and, if it does, whether we are not landed in the morass of subjectivism and solipsism, in which the terms 'truth' and 'fact' become finally evacuated of all meaning.

The idea that dogmatic forms cannot be unalterable because they are the products of a gradual evolution is so common that I will venture to trespass on your patience a little further in connexion with this particular point. Take such an instance of a dogmatic form as the *Homoousion*. I do not dream for a moment that the primitive Church, as it stood on the morrow of Pentecost, used this conception for describing our Lord's relation to the Father: in fact, I do not suppose that it expended over much thought on the exact metaphysical *rationale* of that relation at all. But it does seem to me that it held, in what we should call pictorial and imaginative form, the very same general idea of the Divine Sonship of Christ which was formulated three hundred years later by the Nicene Fathers in the more precise, abstruse, and intellectual terms of the Homoousion formula. One does not of course blame them for not consciously holding the precise conceptual form which was destined to emerge three centuries later, any more than one blames Tertullian for denying the Eternal Generation of the Son *before* the Church had finally settled that this idea was a necessary implicate of the belief in His full Divinity. But, *if* one believes in the Spirit as governing the whole growth of historic Christianity, in its three-fold structure, dogmatic, institutional, and devotional, it follows that the process of dogmatic development is *irreversible*; its direction is ever forwards and not backwards, it must necessarily be wrong and unnatural to go behind what has once been fixed by divinely inspired authority—to attempt to put the hands of the clock back by a return to the simpler and vaguer faith of the Church's infancy, however attractive such a proposal may appear at first sight. In this sense, it is a duty to be sophisticated. I cannot deny myself the (somewhat malicious) satisfaction of observing that from this point of view Modernism, at any rate Continental Modernism, with its cry of ' *Zurück zu Christus* ' (in the sense in which these words are commonly used, that is, as meaning ' *Los von der Kirche, los von Paulus* ') would naturally appear to merit the name of ' reaction ' in its most literal application.

I should, on this ground, challenge the appropriateness of your metaphor of the snake and its old and new skins (p. 10). The Traditionalist would regard the dogmas of the Faith, not as a superficial and periodically changing integument, but as the connected system of vital organs into which the originally simple substance of the embryo has differentiated itself. In the first stages of its existence the embryo is apparently a mere speck of protoplasm, within which no organs can be detected, practically homogeneous throughout; but yet, even at that stage, it contains the potentiality of brain, spinal cord, heart, and lungs, which appear in the course of time, gradually assuming definiteness and consistency, as the working out of a divine idea which was always immanent in the germ. But it does not follow that we can now dispense with lungs because they took some time to develop: and an attempt to return to primitive conditions by a radical simplification of our internal economy would probably prove a peculiarly disastrous experiment in anatomical revision.

Of course, the fact that the outlines and mutual relations of the various organs are potentially fixed from the first, and actually fixed after a comparatively short period of the body's existence, does not condemn it to petrifaction or stagnation, or exclude the possibility of growth and development—on the lines laid down by Nature. No more does the immutability of the conceptual forms once sanctioned by conciliar authority exclude the possibility of a progression, to which no term need or can be set, in the increasing apprehension of the full meaning of their content. If the world lasts so long, future ages may well see more Ecumenical Councils, fresh Creeds and Definitions (I mean, of course, additional to, not contradictory of, the old), and technical theological forms imposed upon such Christian ideas as are still in the undefined and fluid stage, such as that of the Atonement, or of the Inspiration of the Scriptures.

VII

I gather from some words on p. 13 of your paper that you would not altogether repudiate that conception of the immanent Divine Spirit guiding the development of Catholic doctrine which I have endeavoured (very imperfectly and cursorily) to set out above. These words are '. . . (Our young men)[1] are perfectly ready to believe that the good Providence of God presided over the whole evolution.' I welcome this observation, because I want to find points of agreement rather than of difference between us. And on this point it would appear that the difference between the views which we severally take of the Divine guidance of dogmatic evolution is one of degree rather than of kind. I believe that the informing energies of the Holy Spirit penetrated the whole process, as the nerve-force of the body is present in all its functions, so

[1] I am sure you will forgive my entering a respectful but firm protest against the apparent assumption that all 'young men' as such are Modernists. I have had, and still have a large undergraduate acquaintance, which has included many Agnostics, but only three Modernists, of whom one has since become what I should call orthodox.

as to work out, in the Catholic doctrines, the nearest approximation to absolute truth that the human mind is capable of receiving : you, I gather, would conceive this governing and directing activity in a much vaguer and more attenuated sort of way, as keeping Christian doctrine, in a general sense, more or less on the right lines, but by no means safeguarding it against considerable errors in detail. But, if the difference is only one of degree, the gulf between the two positions ought not to be unbridgeable.

To sum up. It seems to me that the situation as between the view represented in your paper and that which I have endeavoured to set out might be roughly sketched as follows :

A. The existence of a permanent body of Christian truth.
  Admitted by both sides.[1]
B. The relativity of the forms in which this permanent body was expressed by the early Creeds and Councils.
  I admit this in some measure, but to nothing like the extent which you desire.
C. The conception of the Holy Spirit, as governing the process whereby the permanent body of Christian ideas was expressed in credal forms.
  You *admit this in some measure, but to nothing like the extent which I desire.*

Can the differences on points B and C be terminated, and if so, how ? I believe that my position on point B— viz. that the categories and forms in which the early Church embodied the deposit of Christian truth are, as a matter of mere fact, such as are inherent in the structure of human thought and the common property of all ages and countries ; and that, so far as they are relative, they

[1] I hope and believe that I am not unduly optimistic in setting this down.

are relative to human thought as such and not to any particular philosophical system—I believe that this position can be amply defended by the ordinary weapons of debate. But I should admit that my view on point C— the belief in the Holy Spirit as guiding the process of dogmatic evolution specifically and in detail, not vaguely and in a general sense—rests upon an intuition. This intuition, whereby the Holy Ghost is seen to be in the Church, is (I should say) analogous to that sense of God in nature which comes fleetingly at times to all, and is possessed in fullest measure by the favoured few, poets, prophets, and mystics. There is a certain sense of the augustness, the sanctity, one might almost say the worshipfulness, of the Church, which appears in the vision of the Ecclesia in Hermas, or in such a phrase as that which occurs in the old Leonine collect ' Ecclesiae tuae *mirabile sacramentum* '. He who has this sense of the sacramental character of the Church—who can see in the historic Society the sacrament, or vehicle, or efficacious sign, of the presence of the Holy Ghost—will not be likely to have much difficulty in recognizing the majestic cadences of the Creeds as the voice of God. The sins, ignorances, and imperfections of the Councils which actually drew up the Creeds and Definitions will be as irrelevant to him as the dust which might settle on the bread of the Lord's Supper would be to the devout communicant. The Reformation in Northern Europe may have had some excellent results : but (on my view) one of its most unfortunate results was the complete or partial destruction of this sense of the Church as the time-garment of the Christ-Spirit, the mystical Body in which the Lord still lives, heals, and suffers, as truly now in Paris, Moscow, or New York as once in Galilee or on Calvary. There are not wanting signs that this sense is slowly reviving in England, and perhaps in Anglo-Saxon Christendom generally ; but its re-creation, as the necessary basis for the re-union of all who love our Lord Jesus Christ in sincerity, will be finally effected by instruments and means belonging to an order other than the purely intellectual.

There are many points of detail in your paper, upon which I could say a great deal, if I had time and space. The ' unification of thought ' is doubtless a splendid ideal : but I do not see how religious and secular thought are to be fused until secular thought itself shows some tendency towards its own inner unification, and ceases to be a jarring chaos of incompatible systems. Otherwise, with what are you going to unify Christianity ? With Bergsonism ? or neo-Hegelianism ? or Spencerism ? or Pragmatism ? or Pan-pneumatism ? But, though much has necessarily been omitted, I have set down, I think, my reflections on the most important questions raised by your paper : and I trust that the length of this note has not unduly tried your patience.

Very sincerely yours,

N. P. WILLIAMS.

DR. SANDAY'S REPLY

MY DEAR WILLIAMS,

I acknowledge warmly the perfect courtesy and considerateness of your letter. I also very much appreciate its great clearness and precision of statement. These are qualities that should enable us to reach a better understanding. It is not to be expected that we should entirely agree; but it will be much if we can reduce the limits between which we seem to disagree. And for this purpose your letter, if I may say so, seems likely to be very helpful.

I will take your points in the order in which they arise, and will add some further comments of my own at the end.

I

I am glad that we can come to terms upon the broad principle of 'continuity and relativity'; and I am also glad that, when you speak of the 'unalterableness' of the Christian Faith, you confine this to the *essential content*, as distinct from the *form* or *expression*. I may perhaps be allowed to remind you of this later, if the occasion should arise, as it possibly may.

II

It is only when we come to the question of 'relativity' that you begin to be conscious of divergence. And I may say here at once that, apart from some small details which would rather overstate my views, I can quite accept the compendious paraphrase into which you throw them. Here again I note the considerable measure of agreement. This covers the propositions which you have numbered

1, 2, 3 b, c. The points that you would 'strenuously deny' are 3 a and the *sequitur* between the three propositions and the conclusion.

I will come to these in a moment; but, before I do so, I ought just to touch upon the points in your statement which rather exaggerate me.

The form of modernism which I desire to defend is distinctly a conservative and (if I may call it so), reverent modernism. For my own part I dislike and deprecate the language into which some modernists are apt to fall that would dismiss impatiently the older forms of statement as 'out of date' and untenable. I would carefully abstain from using several of the expressions which you (not unnaturally) attribute to me. Such would be the phrases, 'inadequate and *pro tanto* untrue', 'the Creeds must in the nature of the case be expected to be wrong', 'the great ideas of the Faith were such as have been outgrown by the modern world'. 'Untrue' (even with the qualification '*pro tanto* untrue'), 'wrong', 'outgrown' (in the sense of discarded), are all words that I should avoid.[1] The attitude of mind to which they correspond is not mine; and, even if it were, they would not be appropriate to the special purpose with which I am writing. I shall have later to try to explain this more fully, and will say no more about it at present.

What you say about '*a priori*' and '*a posteriori*' objections, also needs a word of comment. I do not feel myself tied down to one mode of reasoning rather than another; each has its place according to the context in which it is used. The tendency of your own paper is perhaps rather to lay stress upon the *a priori* side of things. But this is another aspect of our discussion that will come up again presently, and I will not dilate upon it now.

[1] For a fuller exposition of my views on this head, I may perhaps be allowed to refer to an article entitled 'Relative Truth' in *The Modern Churchman* for October–November 1915.

III

I note your remarks under your third head. They are fresh and pointed and deserve full consideration. At the same time, I do not feel that they are inconsistent with the attitude that I should myself wish to adopt in regard to the Creeds. I might describe that attitude in general terms by saying that, where we propound to ourselves the same questions that are raised by the Creeds, especially so far as these questions relate to the metaphysical nature of the Godhead, my own belief is that they are rightly answered in the words of the Creeds. The difference in regard to modern times, as I should put it, is, not that we should answer the same questions differently, but that we should be inclined to put rather different questions. These are not for us the urgent questions that

> rap and knock and enter in our soul,

whether we will or no. We do not challenge the old answers; we assent to them—only perhaps a little less energetically inasmuch as they are less pressing and less the subject of active controversy.

It may help the process of clearing up obscurities, if I take an important example—the doctrine of the Holy Trinity. If I ask how I can best make real to myself this doctrine, I am inclined to reply that I can do so to the best advantage by a study of its history, by observing how as a matter of fact it gradually took shape in the thought of the Early Church. The first impulse to the doctrine was doubtless given by the necessity of distinguishing between the Godhead in the heavens and the Godhead upon earth. This gave rise to the bracketing together of God the Father and God the Son, as in the salutations and elsewhere in St. Paul's Epistles. Then gradually there steals in the use of the triple formula (as in 2 Cor. xiii. 14, 1 Peter i. 2). We enter into the psychology of the Apostolic writers, and try to follow the working of their minds. Then, in like manner, when the Church begins to reflect and philosophize upon its beliefs, we take up a treatise like that of Tertullian ' Against Praxeas ', and we are not surprised to find that the most prominent idea is that of what is called ' the economic Trinity ', the successive ' dispensations ' of the Father, Son, and Holy Spirit. We see how the Church was thus led on to ask if these distinctive operations did not point to some ulterior distinction of being, and to answer that presumably they did. We are conscious that to this day we can give no better answer ; though we hasten to add that, if we venture as far as this, we do so entirely in the spirit of the most profound of the ancient theologians, more particularly St. Augustine : *cum quaeritur, quid tres, magna prorsus inopia humanum laborat eloquium ; dictum est tamen ' tres personae ', non ut illud diceretur, sed ne taceretur* (*De Trin.* v. 9).

The modern Christian feels that he can follow the steps in this process with the deepest respect ; he can adopt the ancient language, and he is ready to fall back upon it as the best that is available for him. But his instinct is all for reticence, and he is glad to think that the pressure for definition from without is less than it has been. The doctrine of the Incarnation is just as urgent as ever it was. The question, What think ye of Christ ? still demands a prompt, clear, and decisive answer. But the further corollaries from this doctrine are not so urgent. The drift of thought is rather away from them, and tends to concentrate itself more upon religious experience and practice. Hence I do not think it is too much to say that the speculative discussions of the past are more in the background of men's minds than in the front of them.

IV

The truths of mathematics stand apart by themselves. The whole system of mathematics is from first to last a creation of the human mind. And what the mind makes, the mind is thoroughly competent to handle. The subject-matter is both finite and definite All that is to be seen of it, the mind can see; it can grasp it, above, beneath, and around. There is no analogy from such comprehension as this to the attitude of the soul towards its God, feeling after Him if haply it may find Him. There is all the difference in the world between truths that are within the compass of the mind and truths that by the nature of the case are beyond it. The study of a finite object is one thing, and the study of an infinite object is another. When all is said, the mind can only resign itself to its limitations.

I am afraid it is a highly paradoxical and precarious position to take up, ' that it is possible to arrive at true conclusions from false, or partially false premises '. I allow that *in appearance* such failures of the mental processes do sometimes happen. I allow that the working of the logical machine is not infallible—that it is not safe to assume that even from sound premises the conclusions that seem to follow will always be sound, and that truth is sometimes arrived at by processes which seem to be faulty. I allow that on these grounds a certain amount of reserve and caution has to be exercised in the conduct of life. But it is quite another thing to erect such exceptional cases into a law, and to act as though the opposite assumption held good.

The rationale of these paradoxical instances appears to be that all reasoning is not conscious; that the sub- and un-conscious processes embrace a wider range of data than the conscious, and are thus sometimes able to correct the more intense activities of conscious reasoning. The seemingly imperfect connexion between premises and conclusion is often simply due to defective analysis.

In any case the fact remains that right processes are the best, if not the only, guarantee we have for right results. To revise and check our processes is the best way of arriving at truth. This is the normal method, and any other is abnormal.

We have the further encouragement of knowing that, as a matter of fact, the processes of reasoning have steadily been improved. In all branches of research advance has been made. The world knows better than it did what kinds of inference are to be trusted and what are not. And this not only imposes on us the duty of going over afresh the old lines of proof, but it also inspires us with growing confidence in following out those trains of reasoning which experience has ratified.

V

I understand that, where rational verification fails, you fall back on the assumption of a Divine presence and influence—in your own words, 'the immanent personal presence of God the Holy Ghost in the Catholic Church' —overruling all defective processes and educing truth even out of that which is recognized as error. I am glad to think that up to a certain point I can go with you here. You are quite right in noticing that I spoke myself of 'the good Providence of God presiding over the whole evolution'. I not only spoke of this but desired, and desire, to lay stress upon it. The belief in this is very real with me.

I had a reason for adopting a rather different mode of expression, though I do not wish to press it to the exclusion of yours. I would rather take your more limited and specific formula as included in mine. My reason for preferring the larger expression was because I wished to cover the whole evolution, pre-Christian as well as Christian I was anxious to take in the whole of the Old Dispensation as well as of the New. Not only have I a strong feeling that we ought to do this, but I also believe that we strengthen our case considerably by doing so.

When all is said, the best proof of Divine intervention and assistance in the spiritual education of the human race is to be found within the four corners of the Bible.

46 *Form and Content in Christian Tradition*

No higher revelation of religious truth has ever been made, or is likely ever to be made, than that which is contained in the Life as well as in the Words of the Lord Jesus Christ. And in all the rest of human history, there are no signs of God's presence and guidance which stand out so boldly as those which cluster thickly round the double line of ascent to and descent from Him.

Along these lines we come from time to time upon concentrated sayings which sum up in classical language the most fundamental principles of religion. ' Hear, O Israel : the Lord our God is one Lord ; and thou shalt love the Lord thy God with all thine heart, and with all thy soul, and with all thy might ' ; ' Thou shalt love thy neighbour as thyself ' ; ' The Lord is slow to anger, and plenteous in mercy, forgiving iniquity and transgression and sin, and will by no means clear the guilty ' ; ' Like as a father pitieth his children, so the Lord pitieth them that fear him ' ; ' This is the covenant that I will make with the house of Israel after those days, saith the Lord ; I will put my law in their inward parts, and in their heart will I write it ; and I will be their God, and they shall be my people ' ; ' The chastisement of our peace was upon him ; and with his stripes we are healed '.

And yet, even in this foundation-laying period in which God seemed nearest to man and in which Divine action upon the human mind appeared at its greatest intensity—even then we can discern certain setbacks or limitations : such as, almost to the end of the Old Testament period, defective grasp upon a future life, a strict law of retaliation, mistaken emphasis on the alleged correspondence between sin and suffering, earthly prosperity and moral desert, and from time to time a startling narrowness of identification between the national cause of Israel and the cause of God.

But if the pre-Christian stage of preparation, though in many ways a time of intense inspiration, was subject to drawbacks such as these, still less can it be said that the later periods of Church History have been exempt from them. We may mark off three distinct stages : (*a*) the period of the Undivided Church ; (*b*) the Middle Ages ; (*c*) the great break-up of Christian Unity and its sequel. Let us grant that, on the whole, a fairly optimistic view is possible of the first of these stages ; however thick the traces may be in it of ' all too human ' infirmities, theoretical and practical, it may be reasonable to detect a Divine overruling in the broad formulation of Christian doctrine. But, whatever allowance may be made for this, it must be difficult to maintain as much for either of the periods which followed. Ideal elements were not wanting in the Middle Ages ; but the upshot of the period was such an accumulation of abuses and corruptions as to call for drastic reformation. And this reformation, in its turn, so broke up the unity of the Church of Christ that combined and effective action of the Church as a whole is no longer possible. It must be regarded as suspended, until the conditions are once again more favourable.

It is for these reasons and because of these drawbacks that I am afraid I cannot follow you in the picture that you draw of the present position of Christian Doctrine. As a picture, it is beautiful and attractive. But my feeling about it is that it is all in the air ; it is out of touch with the workaday world ; it is a work of the imagination, an ' unsubstantial pageant ', neither verified nor capable of verification. You yourself describe it as reached by an ' intuition '. But does not that really mean ' assumed without proof ' ? What assurance have we that it corresponds to the reality ?

It seems to me that, so long as we keep to broad lines and to general statements, a fair case may be made out for tracing the hand of God in history, and for the belief that the broad outlines of the Christian Creed are what He would have them to be. But when the attempt is made to go beyond this and to maintain that each minute detail remains true in precisely the same sense in which it was held fourteen or fifteen or sixteen centuries ago, then I must needs think that the contention goes beyond what we have warrant for. I find it hard to reconcile with the inevitable amount of change that I see going on in the world around me.

I would venture to generalize a step further. There is, as far as I can see, no exception to the law that 'we have our treasure in earthen vessels'; in other words, that Divine communications of every kind are mediated to man through men, through human faculties, with all their weaknesses and limitations adhering to them. Man is privileged to *co-operate* with God; He is συνεργὸς Θεοῦ. But that never means that His own nature ceases to be what it is. If it did, he would cease to be a free agent; he would be a passive instrument, and not an agent at all.

We see this in every field; in the whole Christian life of prayer and answers to prayer, in the life of individuals singly and in the mass. The genuinely human element may be increased or diminished, but it is never eliminated. This means that a partial control from above of human thought and action enters into the scheme of things, but a complete control does not enter into it. I think I may say, no control so complete as to satisfy the conditions which your view would require.

VI

It is true that different parts of the Creed are on a rather different footing. And I am not sure that we have not to some extent been playing at cross purposes about it. Your argument has had reference mainly to what I may call the metaphysical or ontological aspects of the Creeds, whereas I have had chiefly in mind the statements that would come rather under the head of history. I gladly admit that what you have said about the essential simplicity of the ontological statements is much to the point and well deserves to be borne in mind. I have said already that I do not wish to call in question any of these statements. I do not think there is one to which I should wish to offer anything that is in the nature of contradiction. I fully believe that, as far as I can judge, the ultimate formulations accepted by the Church were always in the right direction. It is just in this that I am prepared to see Divine guidance and overruling. There was, if we may say so, an instinct at work in the Church which out of seemingly unpromising conditions and by seemingly unpromising methods was found to lead in the end to what we can recognize as right decisions. All that I would wish to say by way of reserve is that the modern mind has perhaps learnt to be still more on its guard against the dangers of over-definition; it is more aware of its own limitations; and it is specially reluctant to venture too far in its affirmations about God. The famous passage in Hooker (*Eccl. Pol.* I. ii. 2) stands out as a warning that the best divines of the Church of England have always kept well before them. I do not think that there is any danger of their not doing so in future.

It is otherwise with the historical statements embodied in the Creeds. So far as these are historical, they are on the same footing as all history. We do not write history now in the same way in which it was written two centuries ago. And if this holds good for the history of Greece and Rome, it must also hold good for the history of Palestine. We cannot mark off one small corner, and apply to it different methods and principles from those which we apply to all the rest. As a matter of fact, the history of the Old Testament period has been, or is in process of being, rewritten on these methods and principles. The only remaining question is how far they are similarly applicable to the New Testament period. And it seems to me that we have no choice but to go forward frankly upon the same lines.

In the end what determines the interpretation of the New Testament will determine also the interpretation of the Creeds. The New Testament supplies the data that are worked up in the Creeds. It follows that, if there is a progressive reinterpretation of the one, the same thing must hold good of the other.

VII

It is here that the work of the modernist, and especially of the modernist scholar, comes in. His supreme desire and effort is to see things as they really are, and to make his life and thought all of a piece. As it is, he has no confidence that he is doing this. So long as he merely reproduces the traditional story, he is haunted by a sense that the ground beneath his feet is no more secure than it is in the case of other traditional stories. He feels that he must go behind this, and go behind it methodically and systematically; he must bring to bear upon it all the resources of historical and critical experience.

That does not mean that he must pin himself down to any particular set of conclusions. The search for truth in these matters is certainly at the present time some way from finality. The virtue is in the search, rather than (as yet) in the results of the search. As we look back over the investigations of the last fifty or sixty years, what they seem to have done is to have turned a strong searchlight first upon this and then upon that point in the real sequence of the New Testament history; the points are real points, and to have become conscious of them is a genuine step in advance; but it would be another thing to say that up till now we have succeeded in setting them all in their just proportions and correlating them exactly with each other. The movement is a progressive movement, and we must be content if we can make way by slow degrees.

And yet, after all, these studies in which Christian scholars have been employed, important as they are and near as they are to the fountain-head, belong to the field of externals; they have to do rather with expression than with that which is expressed. They are not themselves the full spiritual meaning, which comes to light through them. The reason why these studies of which I have been speaking are pursued so eagerly as they are is in the hope of disengaging more and more of that full spiritual meaning.

And I myself believe that this inner meaning will not be found to be essentially different from what it has been all along. I would not say that it exactly is, but it certainly lies behind, the theology of St. Paul and St. John. Even those first and greatest of all theologies require some discrimination between form and content; even they embody features which are taken from the current thought of the time; even they involve a certain process of translation and interpretation when we attempt to express them in the forms most natural to ourselves. But translation and interpretation are a different thing from essential change.

I gladly accept your own expressive image (p. 35), which becomes most expressive when we think of the subject of it as human. The child, the boy, the youth, the man, differ to some extent, though never wholly, in outward physiognomy; but the inner personality, the vital organs, are one and the same.

I suppose that few philosophical problems are more difficult than the precise definition of that which constitutes identity. Your own conception of the identity of Christian doctrine in the present and in the past implies such a definition. But I am afraid I must ask for a greater amount of latitude than you seem inclined to grant. When you say that 'each doctrine, as it took shape, assumed precisely that *form* which the Holy Spirit foresaw would most perfectly preserve the essential *content* till the end of time' (p. 32 *sup.*), it seems to me that you are claiming too much. You are not content with assuming that the essential content remains the same, but you go on to assert that the outward form or expression must be equally immutable. I find it hard to reconcile this language with what is implied in your own analogies. Does it allow for the inevitable processes of growth ? If the world were constructed on mechanical principles—if the thoughts in men's minds were like coins in a box—then, one could believe that what was handed in at one point could be taken out in precisely the same condition at another. But that is surely too simple a way of looking at it. We have to do with living minds, and with a succession of living minds. Under such conditions, the more natural analogy is surely that of organic growth. And the essential characteristic of organic growth is that identity and change are perfectly balanced ; the single particles are in perpetual flux, but the living being, the person, remains always the same. We meet a friend, let us say, after an interval of ten years, and we see at a glance that he is at once the same and not the same ; it is hard to tell where the likeness ends and the unlikeness begins ; there is the subtlest possible identity, and yet the subtlest possible difference, in every feature. The proportions of likeness and unlikeness vary with the individual. To one, the first words of one's greeting are, ' I should hardly have known you ; ' to another, ' You are not altered a bit.' And yet, in both cases alike, we take up the thread of our common past as if it had never been broken.

That is surely the law of life, the pattern on which life is made and to which all its phases conform. The history of Christian belief and Christian doctrine is no exception. It seems to me that you are trying to stereotype both beyond the point to which they can be or ought to be stereotyped.

VIII

That is where—be it said with all respect—it seems to me that you are wrong. This idea of an infallible Church with an unalterable body of doctrine : what better foundation has it in the last resort than that you would like to think it true ? There have been and are many claimants to infallibility. But the previous question ought to be asked : Is there any such thing as infallibility among the sons of men ? ' By their fruits ye shall know them.'

Does not the theory which you advocate presuppose an idealized—and even a highly idealized—view of history ? All idealism no doubt has its attractions. But, when I think of this, I am reminded of an analogous case in the Old Testament. The Book of Chronicles—we remember that in the Hebrew it is a single book—is also very largely in its essence an ideal construction. It is a rewriting of Judaean history on certain definite principles. The author is strongly impressed with one of the current articles of Jewish belief, the strict correspondence of outward prosperity with moral and religious desert, the doctrine that the wicked are punished and the righteous rewarded even in this life. The narrative is cut out to fit this doctrine, just as a coat is cut to fit the wearer. Awkward and intractable facts (like the sins of David and Solomon) are studiously omitted ; and, where further details are needed to make good the moral, they are duly supplied. Then again, the author is also an enthusiast for the fully developed ceremonial of his own day, and he reads this back into the times of David and Solomon ; he describes the great functions of their reigns as if they had been conducted in accordance with the fullest later standards ; and in other ways he is always levelling up the earlier with the later usage and depicting things, not as they actually were, but as he conceives that they ought to have been. He is a good man, but with the goodness of his own time, and he corrects the older authorities in accordance with this. But, whatever else he may be, he is not a trustworthy historian.

In sharp contrast with this book are two others—one probably written a hundred years or so earlier, and the other somewhat later—the Books of Job and Ecclesiastes.

As compared with the author of Chronicles, the authors of both these books might be called realists. Their one endeavour is to see things as they are. They will not go on repeating the old phrases, unless they are sure that they are true. The doctrine of the unfailing prosperity of the righteous and penalizing of the wicked is a stumbling-block to them. They see that it does not correspond to the facts, and they will not represent things otherwise than as they see them. They will not 'speak unrighteously for God' or 'talk deceitfully for him' (Job xiii. 7). 'The Preacher' goes further still; he is not only a realist but a pessimist; he does not shrink from saying what he believes to be true, however paradoxical it may sound. Yet his temper is austere and grave, and he is resigned not to know more than is revealed to him.

It is not surprising that there should have been some hesitation about admitting this last book within the Canon. Yet I think that we have much reason to be glad that it was admitted. It represents a type of mind and character which deserves to be consecrated to God's service. We may take it as an illustration of the truth that 'God fulfils Himself in many ways'.

It is really for a further recognition of this truth that I have been pleading. I do not take it amiss that you do not see your way to grant me all that I have asked for. In matters such as this *rapprochements* are not to be forced. We must wait in patience until they come about spontaneously and naturally.

Believe me,
Always yours sincerely,
W. SANDAY.

MR. N. P. WILLIAMS'S SECOND LETTER

MY DEAR DR. SANDAY,

Permit me to thank you very sincerely for your letter, and to express my gratification that we have been able to discover so much common ground. I gather from certain expressions in your letter that the extent to which you would go with me is greater even than I had hoped: and I am indeed glad that this is so. In this paper I propose to examine the divergences that remain, to reply to the criticisms which you have directed against my position, and, if possible, to trace our remaining divergences in respect of conclusions down to their ultimate root in differences of fundamental assumptions. The methods and canons of right reasoning are the same for all: so also are the *data* of sense-experience: when, therefore, two equally reasonable people (if I may without presumption bracket myself with you in this way) come to different conclusions in respect of the same subject-matter, it must necessarily be because they are using different axioms, or (as Plato would say) different ἀρχαὶ ἀνυπόθετοι. All chains of proof depend ultimately upon assumptions which themselves neither require nor are capable of proof; otherwise ratiocination of every kind would, when analysed, dissolve away into an infinite regress. It is therefore rigorously certain that our differences can be reduced to differences of fundamental, unproved, and unprovable assumption; and the laying bare of these divergent ἀρχαί is the task which I shall propose to myself in this paper. I could, of course, did time and space permit, write a running commentary upon the whole of your letter; there are parts of it with which I heartily agree, parts to which I assent with rather less enthusiasm, or which I do not feel called upon seriously to challenge, though I might myself wish to word them differently—and parts with which I must needs disagree *in toto*. It will conduce both to brevity and to clearness if I confine myself to the consideration of these latter.

I

I think it is not unfair to say that your letter, on the whole, vindicates the correctness of my diagnosis of the situation as between the views which you have expressed on the subject of the creeds and their authority, and those which I have tried to expound. I expressed the opinion (you will remember) that the *fons et origo* of the cleavage between us was to be found in the divergent opinions which we held as to the extent to which the guidance of the Holy Spirit controlled (and presumably still controls) the evolution of Christian dogma. And I suggested that, whilst this idea was accepted by both of us, you did not appear to admit it ' to anything like the extent which I desired '. I am, of course, only too glad to learn that this phrase was in your opinion over-strong. But I gather from your subsequent remarks that there *is* a real divergence, though not so great as I had feared—and that this divergence is the fount, or one of the founts, of all our subsequent differences. You say, indeed (on p. 45), that you do not wish to challenge my phrase about ' the immanent personal presence of God the Holy Ghost in the Catholic Church ', and prefer to take the idea for which it stands as included in your own more comprehensive conception of Divine Providence as presiding over the whole course of Judaeo-Christian evolution. But (without any wish to lay stress on points of difference, and actuated merely by the desire to expose the logic of the matter) I am constrained to observe that you almost immediately take back with one hand a good deal of what you seem to be giving me with the other. For you bring against my view of Church authority in doctrinal matters a number of criticisms, some of which, at least, if they could be sustained, would, to my mind, have the effect of upsetting it altogether. My first task must, therefore, be that of replying to these criticisms : when that has been done, I may proceed to lay bare a second difference of fundamental assumption, which, equally with the first, seems to lie at the root of the schism between the Traditionalist and the Modernist tendencies in Christian thought.

II

The first criticism which I will discuss is directed against my admission that the fundamental postulate of the Catholic system, viz. the belief in the guiding presence of the Holy Spirit in the Church, or, more briefly, the belief in the 'infallibility' of the Church, rests frankly upon an intuition. You ask 'Does not this mean, assumed without proof ? ' To which I reply, Of course it does. From the view-point of uncompromising orthodoxy, this belief is the fundamental assumption, which must in the nature of things be both unproved and unprovable, because it is itself the *prius* which makes any kind of proof possible—the ἀρχὴ ἀναπόδεικτος which is the necessary presupposition of all solid and reliable ἀπόδειξις in the domain of Christian doctrine. You are at liberty, if you will—and are able—to disprove this fundamental assumption of traditional dogmatic theology by showing that the Church has laid down as of faith statements which are now certainly known to be untrue : though I cannot say that I have much fear of your being able to do so. But I do not see that you can reasonably object to what is admittedly put forward as an ἀρχὴ ἀναπόδεικτος merely for *being* ἀναπόδεικτος. You might as well criticize the Laws of Thought, or the axioms of geometry, for being 'assumed without proof'— which is exactly what they are. After all, the other sciences are all based upon assumptions which in the last analysis are seen to be themselves incapable of proof : otherwise (as I said above) all scientific demonstration, whether deductive or inductive, would be a chain hanging from nothing, a ladder losing itself in the mists of an infinite regress. The world may rest upon an elephant, and the elephant upon a tortoise : but the tortoise must be provided with a ποῦ στῶ which needs no further support. This is most obviously clear in the case of the deductive sciences, such as mathematics : but it is really none the less true in the case of the empirical sciences, which presuppose such utterly unprovable postulates as the existence of an external world, and the reliability of sense-perception. In the spheres of conduct and of aesthetic feeling, the same is the case ; the scales of moral and aesthetic values, which all reasoning about the Good or the Beautiful necessarily presupposes, are given us by the ethical and aesthetic senses respectively —that is, by ethical and aesthetic 'intuition'—and not by ratiocination. Even in the practical life of every day, we find ourselves at every turn acting upon principles of which we are certain, though they cannot be proved : which are given us by the Practical, and not by the Pure Reason : we have to walk, in great measure, by faith and not by sight. And if every other domain of human thought, feeling, and action possesses and presupposes its own fundamental and indemonstrable first principles, why need it be thought a thing incredible that religion in general (and the Christian religion in particular) should possess its own ἀρχαὶ ἀναπόδεικτοι, as the starting-point for all subsequent ἀπόδειξις ? You would not deny (I imagine) that the great ideas of religion in general —God, Freedom, Immortality—are matters of intuition rather than of demonstration : you would hardly maintain that the stock arguments for the existence of God have been unaffected by Kant's destructive criticism, or that the being and attributes of the Godhead can be 'proved' from the *data* of sense-experience as easily and certainly as Paley supposed. For the believing soul, the reality of a loving and all-merciful Father and Creator rests primarily upon intuition, or spiritual experience, or the Divine gift of Faith (they are all names for the same ineffable interior sense of God's presence), and not upon reasoning, whether deductive or inductive : and for the vast majority of Christian believers this sense of the reality of God is indissolubly knit up with the sense of Him in Christ, reconciling the world to Himself, and of Christ in the Church and the Sacraments, healing, restoring, sanctifying. I venture to claim that you cannot, in logic, disparage the idea of ' intuition ' of Divine things, without destroying the basal foundations of religious conviction altogether.

You draw a contrast between my view, based frankly on ' intuition ', and your own rather vaguer view of the extent to which the Holy Spirit presided over the whole course of Judaeo-Christian evolution, for which you claim to find ' a real warrant in history '. You suggest, a little further on, that I am going beyond the warrant of history in pressing this Divine guidance, during the Christian period, to the point of endowing the Christian Church with ' infallibility '. I imagine that I should not be representing your contention unfairly if I summarized it as claiming that your view rests upon a scientific, or more or less scientific, or exact, *induction* from the facts of history, whereas mine rests upon an unverifiable *intuition*. And you instance some of the great texts of the Old Testament as proofs of the reality of this Divine guidance, understood in a general sense. But I must point out that your induction, if closely analysed, really rests at every point upon an intuition at least as unverifiable as mine—it is, in fact, a whole series of such intuitions rather than an induction properly so called. An example will explain what I mean. You quote the texts ' The Lord is slow to anger and plenteous in mercy. . . .', ' Like as a father pitieth his children, so the Lord pitieth them that fear him ': and you claim them as proofs of 'Divine intervention and assistance in the spiritual education of the human race'. This argument, I imagine, really amounts to the following—'These great texts, scattered at intervals throughout the pages of the Old Testament, are manifestly Divine : we can, therefore, infer from them that a Divine force must have been at work behind and beneath the course of Israelitish history, bearing it ever upwards until the Old Covenant culminated in the New ; and the same induction can be made with even greater certitude from the facts of the Gospels and the subsequent history of Christendom.' Yes, but on what does your premiss rest, viz. the proposition that 'these great texts are manifestly Divine' ? Is not this proposition 'assumed without proof', and does it not frankly 'rest upon an intuition' ? To put the question in another way, how do you know that God, or the Absolute Reality, or (to use Herbert Spencer's phrase) 'the Infinite and Eternal Energy from which all things proceed', is of the same moral nature as that commended in these texts ? From the point of view of pure reason and rigorous proof, the statements that 'The Lord is plenteous in mercy' and, fatherlike, 'pitieth them that fear him', are by no means self-evident. On the contrary, if I did not (through no merits of my own) possess the intuition, or the 'gift of Faith', I should be strongly inclined—looking at the waste and futility of nature, the 'vanity' to which creation is manifestly subjected on the one hand, and the tragedies of human history, the immense catalogue of man's crimes, cruelties, and sufferings, and the seas of blood and tears which are drenching Europe at the present moment, on the other —to conceive the ultimate Reality as a non-moral and impersonal Absolute. It is useless to object 'But that would be pure cynicism': we are, for the moment, concerned simply with what can be *proved* : and from the point of view of rigorous proof the cynic can make out just as a good a case for an atheistic view of history as you and I can for a theistic view. It is Faith, or spiritual intuition, alone, which assures us that God is Love : that the prophets of old, who discerned infinite tenderness and fatherly affection and compassion at the heart of the universe, were not deceived ; that the tragedies of nature and of human history (in so far as they are not directly due to the perverted will of man) must be susceptible of some explanation transcending our present faculties, some reconciliation with the infinite power and goodness of the world's Creator. The first stanza of ' In Memoriam ' contains the root of the whole matter—

> Strong Son of God, immortal Love,
> Whom we, that have not seen thy face,
> By Faith, and Faith alone, embrace,
> *Believing where we cannot prove*.[1]

I have said enough, I hope, to show, not merely that you cannot justly make it a matter of reproach to me that my view is frankly based upon an intuition, but that your own, somewhat vaguer, view is equally based upon intuition—and, indeed, upon the same intuition, or an intuition of the same facts—only, as I should hold, of a somewhat imperfect character. But I cannot forbear

---

[1] You will have gathered from the foregoing what kind of reply I should give to your observation on p. 52, the rhetorical force of which I fully recognize—' This idea of an infallible Church with an unalterable body of doctrine : what better foundation has it in the last resort than that you would like to think it true ? ' If you will allow me, for the sake of the argument, momentarily to assume a standpoint which is not in reality mine, I might retort with another question— ' This idea of a " personal God "—of an illimitable supra-mundane Power, self-conscious, righteous, and loving, interfering in the affairs of men, and shaping the course of human history towards some far-off divine goal—what better foundation has it in the last resort than that you would like to think it true ? ' I imagine that your reply to the latter question would, *mutatis mutandis*, serve equally well as my reply to the former.

from driving this contention home by pointing out that you have expressly admitted it in several places, only using a different word to designate the very same mode of spiritual activity which I have called 'intuition'. That word is 'feeling'. I need only instance such passages as (in your first paper) the quotation from Matthew Arnold about the difference between 'what we say we feel' and 'what we think we feel' and 'what we feel indeed', or the statement on p. 13, 'A great deal [of the living beliefs of the present day] may remain as a matter of *feeling* rather than of words.' It is surely not unfair to claim that the difference between 'intuition' and 'feeling' is, again, solely one of terminology. By the word 'intuition' I do not mean to suggest that the indefinable faculty of spiritual apprehension, whereby the soul is aware of God in Nature and in the Church, is purely intellectual; nor (I imagine) do you, by the word 'feeling', mean that this faculty is merely a function of the 'vegetal soul' or of the nervous system. I doubt whether it is necessary, for our present purposes, or indeed ultimately possible, to define the nature of 'Faith' in terms of exact psychology; probably it involves the activity of every 'part' of the soul (if Aristotle's language may be employed for rough-and-ready expression), thought, will, and emotion alike.

But if this be so—if my 'intuition' and your 'feeling' are substantially the same thing—it is possible to expose, with great clearness, the root of the difference between us. I have a peculiarly vital and intense apprehension, or intuition, or sense, or feeling, of the presence of God in Christ and Christ in the Church; this enables me to lay aside all further anxieties and worries, and to trust absolutely to the formal decisions of the Church as being the voice of God (of course, speaking, as explained in my first letter, through human *media* and in human modes of expression). You, on the other hand, have the same sense or apprehension of God in the history of the Jewish and Christian Churches; only in a somewhat weakened or attenuated form. Consequently, you are not able to throw yourself, with absolute confidence, back upon the Creeds and Ecumenical Definitions, as the nearest equivalent to absolute truth at which the human mind is ever likely to arrive: you cannot simply repose in the deliveries of orthodox Christian tradition without more ado: you require to be reassured at every turn, by a special and separate 'intuition' or 'feeling', that each particular article of the Creed really does correspond to absolute reality—and, I gather, in a few cases (notably those of the historical statements in the Creeds, of which more presently) this special reassurance is not forthcoming. A single intuition, which assures me of the truth of Catholic Christianity as a whole, is enough for me; having once, so to speak, got inside the Catholic system, I have nothing further to do (so far as the essentials of faith are concerned) than to ascertain what, as a matter of fact, are its contents. Having once taken the plunge, I can commit myself without hesitation to the broad main stream of historic Christianity, and allow it to bear me whithersoever it will. You, on the other hand, are not prepared to take the plunge without reservations; you seem to desire, as it were, whilst immersing yourself in the stream as much as possible, to keep one foot on the bank. The Modernist may regard this as a safer attitude, but it is certainly not so comfortable as mine; and, after all, 'nothing venture, nothing have'. A Faith which does not involve taking risks is no Faith at all.

To sum up. My reply to your first criticism may be summarized as follows:

1. All chains of proof must start somewhere—they presuppose indemonstrable ἀρχαί which must necessarily be given by immediate intuition and not by ratiocination.
2. The great ideas of religion—God, Freedom, Immortality—are conspicuous instances of such inde-

monstrable ἀρχαί—the so-called 'proofs' of their reality are now generally regarded as inconclusive, from the point of view of rigorous reasoning.
3. You yourself really seem to admit the principle of 'intuition' by the use which you make of the term 'feeling'.
4. In fact, 'intuition' or 'feeling' seems to play an even greater part in your system than it does in mine: because *I* merely invoke the idea of 'intuition' at the beginning of things, to give me my first principle—God in Christ and Christ in the Church—the peg from which my chain of proof is to hang: having obtained my ἀρχή by means of 'intuition', I can then proceed by way of pure ratiocination, or rather of mere inspection of the facts; I have only to inform myself as to what the deliveries of orthodox tradition actually are. Whereas you not merely invoke 'intuition' or 'feeling' at the beginning of things, but keep on invoking it all through; not merely does your chain depend from the peg of 'intuition', but half of its links appear to be 'intuitions' as well.

III

The second criticism with which I have to deal is contained in the words 'Does not the theory which you advocate presuppose an idealized and even a highly idealized view of history?' You will forgive me if I paraphrase this somewhat bluntly, and substitute for 'an idealized view of history' the words 'a view of history which is, as a matter of fact, not strictly true—which has been, whether consciously or unconsciously, constructed in accordance with preconceived ideas and not with facts'; because that, after all (if we are willing to call a spade a spade) is what the expression 'an idealized view of history' really means. And the comparison which you institute between the view of early Christian history which you attribute to me and the view of early Hebrew history which underlies the Book of Chronicles bears out this interpretation of your words. But can you substantiate this somewhat general indictment ? To what *historical* proposition have I committed myself which can be certainly shown to be untrue ? Let me quote the sentence in which I endeavoured to summarize the ἀρχὴ ἀναπόδεικτος of traditional dogmatic theology :

'That great assumption is the belief in the immanent personal presence of God the Holy Ghost in the Catholic Church, working in and through the processes of its life, overruling the turbulence and ambition of its leaders, sifting out the categories which are of permanent value, and belong to the essential structure of human thought, from the *detritus* of merely temporary and local thought-forms, and inspiring the whole *nexus* of dogmatic development so intimately and pervasively that each doctrine, as it took shape, assumed precisely that *form* which the Holy Spirit foresaw would most perfectly preserve the essential *content* till the end of time.'

You will observe that this hypothesis has reference solely to what I may call the reverse, as opposed to the obverse, side of the historical process—to the Divine influences which were at work beneath the surface of the stream of events, rather than to the events themselves —to the hidden strings which moved the marionettes, rather than to the marionettes or their movements. In all sympathetic historical study—that is, in all study of the past which professes to be more than a mere cataloguing of desiccated names and dates—we can distinguish clearly between (1) the process of ascertaining the facts, and (2) the spiritual and moral evaluation of the facts when ascertained. And my hypothesis belongs avowedly to the latter sphere of thought and not to the former. I desired, and desire, expressly to 'guard myself against any suspicion of 'idealizing' the actual brute facts. I never pretended that Jerome and Cyril were conspicuous for meekness and controversial good manners, that empresses and court favourites had nothing to do (on the earthly plane) with the triumph of those opinions which eventually emerged with the stamp of ' orthodoxy ' upon them, or that Ecumenical Councils were invariably models of staid and decorous deportment.

All that my fundamental assumption commits me to is the belief that the whole tangle of motives, good and bad, which underlay the struggles between Sabellian and Tritheist, or Alexandrine and Antiochene—the whole complex of ideas and imaginations, true, half-true, or false, mythical or historical, which filled the minds of the ancient thinkers—was, as a matter of fact, so deftly arranged and imperceptibly guided by the Holy Spirit dwelling in the Church, that truth, or the nearest approximation to truth of which the human mind is capable, emerged. I am only concerned to maintain that what did come out of the crucible of doctrinal controversy was what God willed should come out : I am under no obligation, and have no wish, to make out the actual chemists, their materials, or their methods, to have been better than they were.

IV

This conception of the Holy Spirit guiding the corporate mind of the Christian Ecclesia—in such a way that (through whatever convulsions and struggles) exact truth, or truth as exact as mortals can hope for, was in the long run worked out—naturally leads me to the consideration of the criticism which I will take next in order. It is summarized in three sentences on p. 48:

> ' The genuinely human element ' (in the intercourse of man and God) ' may be increased or diminished, but it is never eliminated. This means that a partial control from above of human thought and action enters into the scheme of things, but a complete control does not enter into it. I think I may say, no control so complete as to satisfy the conditions which your view would require.'

I may say at once that I entirely agree with the first two of these sentences. My last section will have shown you that I am very far from claiming that the ' genuinely human element ' was ' eliminated ' from the history of the evolution of dogma : very much the contrary : as I have said, I fully admit its presence. I do not assert that the ' control ' exerted by the Holy Spirit was ' complete ' in the sense that the consciousnesses, or the personalities, of the human agents concerned were temporarily suspended. But the real point at issue comes in the third sentence. I believe that, though the Divine control was very far from being ' complete ' (in the sense of amounting to Pythonic possession or obsession) and though it may have been exerted through the most secret avenues and in the most subtle and impalpable manner possible, there was, nevertheless, just enough of it to preserve the Christian Church from laying down as of faith propositions which were definitely false or misleading (and this is all that ' infallibility '—incapacity for deceiving or being deceived—really means) : you, I gather, do not feel able to postulate even so much ' control ' as would have this effect. But why not ?

Apparently, because there are no *other* instances of such Divine control exerted upon the minds of human beings in order to the formulation of the contents of a Divine revelation in the most perfect manner possible. But why should we expect to find any other instances ? If Christianity really is God's final revelation of Himself to mankind—if it is never destined to be antiquated or superseded —it must be regarded as a phenomenon unique in the history of the human race, and it is, therefore, not to be wondered at that it should present features which cannot be paralleled in other religions. God spake $\pi o \lambda \upsilon \mu \epsilon \rho \hat{\omega} s$ καὶ πολυτρόπως to the Hebrew fathers through the prophets— imperfectly and fragmentarily, through human faculties, with, as you justly observe, all their weaknesses and limitations adhering to them ; but in these last days He has spoken unto us by a Son ; and if we believe that Jesus was, not merely 'the last and greatest of the Hebrew prophets', but the omnipotent Son of God Himself, it is, surely, to be expected that the religion which He founded should reflect on all its sides the uniqueness of His Person. At any rate, it is not *a priori* incredible that the Incarnation should have made a difference, not merely to man's moral, but to his mental possibilities : that the gift of sanctifying grace to heal the disorders of the will should have been accompanied by the gift of a clear and unwavering light to dispel the darkness of the intellect. It is, therefore, no argument against the reality of a quality alleged to belong to the Christian Church (in this instance, that of ' infallibility ' in the formulation of revealed truth) to urge that this quality did not belong to the Jewish Church, or to any less perfect religious system.

Formally, these considerations seem to me to be a sufficient answer to your criticism. I do not, of course, mean that they prove, taken by themselves, that the Church really *is* ' infallible ', but merely that they cancel this particular *a priori* objection to the hypothesis of its ' infallibility '. But I am unwilling to leave the matter on a merely ' formal ' basis, as I seem to see the possibility of clearing away one or two misunderstandings which may arise, or have arisen.

It may be objected that the degree of ' uniqueness ' which I have above attributed to Christianity, drives a wedge between the Old Covenant and the New, assumes a gulf or discontinuity between them which is inherently improbable. To this I would reply that I postulate, not discontinuity, but only such a difference between the two stages of God's revelation as is involved in the conception of a real Incarnation of God intervening between them. All else that was permanently true or valuable in Judaism ran continuously on into Christianity, only transfigured and raised to its highest possible power by its assumption into the mystical life which the Redeemer lives in His Church, the 'extension' of His Incarnation. There seems no reason, therefore, in the nature of things, why the guidance of the Spirit, which had bestowed upon the Jewish Church a vague and (so to speak) formless apprehension of some of the mysteries of the Divine Essence, should not have been, at Pentecost, enormously increased and intensified, in such a way as to guide the Christian Church into 'all truth'—all truth, that is, which the human mind is capable of receiving and assimilating : nor do I see any reason why God should not have made provision that the increased range of man's knowledge about Himself should be accompanied by an increase of certainty and precision in the intellectual apprehension and formulation of that knowledge. Nor, to my mind, would this involve any unnatural dislocation or inconcinnity in the smooth and continuous working of the Divine οἰκονομία. Perhaps you will permit me a somewhat commonplace illustration. There is no substantial discontinuity between the flame of a gas-jet turned low, so that only a blue spark hovers above the burner, and the contents of the room are only dimly and in general outline discernible, and the same flame turned high, so that the room is flooded with light, and its contents are clearly seen.

It is possible, further, that I may still be supposed to conceive the guidance exercised by the Holy Spirit over the Church in a coarsely mechanistic manner : that my references to the authority of Ecumenical Councils may expose me to the suspicion of believing in that conception of the inspiration of ecclesiastical authority which is satirized in the somewhat blasphemous *mot* quoted by Sarpi with reference to the Council of Trent (a *mot* which reverence forbids me to repeat). It is therefore worth while observing that, on the view that I am advocating, it is the Church as a whole, the 'Spirit-bearing body' as a whole, which is the ultimate authority. The ecumenicity of Ecumenical Councils resides precisely in this, that their formulations were subsequently accepted by the whole Church. For instance, the first Council of Constantinople, which taught that the Holy Spirit was a distinct Hypostasis within the Godhead, and not a mere impersonal effluence from it, could not and did not, whilst it was sitting, claim to be Ecumenical in the sense of being genuinely representative, in regard to its membership, of the whole Church: inasmuch as none but Eastern bishops attended it. It *became* Ecumenical through the universal acceptance of its decrees by the Christian society in all its parts. There is, therefore, no idea of a supernaturally-possessed body of men, or a majority of them, miraculously hitting off the ideal expression of the truth as it were in a moment; there is no Christian analogue to the Rabbinical figment of the *Bath Qol*. The Catholic hypothesis merely asserts that when rival thinkers or schools of thinkers (or, in some cases, rival Councils) had, after years of debate, worked out different forms for the embodiment of the same content, the vast inarticulate consciousness of the Universal Church was slowly and gradually led, by the viewless influence of the Holy Spirit dwelling within it, to adopt that particular form which God knew to be, for finite intellects, the best preservative of the content in question.[1] There is a sentence on p. 49 of your letter, which, if I were allowed to apply it to *all* the clauses of the Creeds, 'historical' as well as 'ontological', and to read it with my own emphasis attached to particular words, would represent very fairly what I mean. 'I fully believe', you say, 'that, so far as I can judge, the ultimate

---

[1] I may say at this point that I quite agree with your view, expressed on p. 47, that since the Reformation (and indeed since the Great Schism of 1054), owing to the loss of external unity, the normal action of the Church must be regarded as 'suspended, until the conditions are once more favourable'. But this fact does not seem to me, in itself, to cast any doubt upon the conclusions at which the Church arrived before 1054, when it was able to act normally.

formulations accepted by the Church were always in the right direction. It is just in this that I am prepared to see Divine guidance and overruling. There was, if we may say so, an instinct at work in the Church which out of seemingly unpromising conditions and by seemingly unpromising methods was found to lead in the end to what we can recognize as right decisions.' Compare this with the sentence which I have written above—' I believe that though the Divine control was far from being "complete" . . . there was, nevertheless, just enough of it to preserve the Christian Church from laying down as of faith propositions which were definitely false or misleading.' I do not think it is too much to claim that the difference between the conceptions of ' Divine guidance ' expressed in these two sentences is infinitesimal. The real question at issue is whether this ' Divine guidance ' covers both the ' historical ' and the ' ontological ' elements in traditional orthodoxy : and of this, more presently.

V

Your fourth criticism is expressed in the following words—'(The picture that you draw of the present position of Christian doctrine) as a picture, is beautiful and attractive. But my feeling about it is that it is all in the air ; it is out of touch with the work-a-day world ; it is a work of the imagination, an " unsubstantial pageant ", neither verified nor capable of verification.' I will reply as briefly as possible.

To the objection that my view is out of touch with the work-a-day world it should be sufficient to reply that it is, as a matter of fact, held by two-thirds of Christendom at the present day. You have accused me above of maintaining a ' highly paradoxical and precarious position ' in pointing out, what is a commonplace of formal logic, that it is possible to educe true conclusions from false premisses ;[1]

[1] I had not the smallest idea of ' erecting these exceptional cases into a law' (p. 44). It would indeed be sheer unreason to contend that

I can only say that in my opinion it is a far more startling paradox to contend that the Catholic view, which for centuries has been, and still is, the stay and consolation of countless millions of every age, social class, colour, race, and language, is ' out of touch '—and that a view which is comparatively modern, and only held by scholars and persons of trained intellect, is ' in touch '—with ' the work-a-day world '. On this point I am content to let the facts speak for themselves.

As for the allegation that the Catholic hypothesis is ' neither verified nor capable of verification ', I am quite willing to admit that *complete* intellectual verification is as little to be looked for in the case of Catholicism in particular, as it is in the case of Christianity or of Theism in general. I think, indeed, that this hypothesis can be very largely verified, even intellectually; I should certainly claim that it fits the facts of history at least as closely and satisfactorily as, let us say, Harnack's ' secularization-hypothesis '. But, in the case of religious doctrines, the only kind of ' verification ' which can afford convincing proof, or proof which will be convincing to the individual, is practical verification within the sphere of the moral and religious life. I will not pursue this subject at length, because it is of such a profound and intimate nature : but those who have striven to live the Christian life on the lines which are common to the historic Churches of East and West, persevering in the use of penance and

' all faulty processes of reasoning result in true conclusions', and any one who acted on this principle would, no doubt, soon find himself placed under restraint. I merely wished to point out the obvious fact that ' some faulty processes *have* resulted in true conclusions ', and to suggest that, in consequence, the conclusions reached by the primitive Fathers cannot be condemned off-hand merely because some of their premisses were erroneous. Of course, I did not suppose that this contention established the *truth* of their conclusions : I relied for that upon the assumption, which you afterwards proceed to discuss, of the ' immanent personal presence of God the Holy Ghost in the Catholic Church '.

communion, and endeavouring to make the 'Communion of Saints' a living reality to themselves, will know what I mean.

I do not think that the cogency of this interior verification, for those who have experienced it, is disturbed by the fact that grace can be and is given apart from the historic Church and Sacraments : there is the principle *Deus non alligatur mediis, sed homo*, to cover this fact. It may be objected [1] that such an experiential verification can be claimed with as much justice by those who stand apart, at varying degrees of distance, from the great central structure of historic and sacramental Christianity : that the Quaker and the Salvationist can claim that their respective theological positions are guaranteed by their extra- or non-sacramental experience. In a sense, I should agree with this contention : that is, I should quite admit that the Salvationist can legitimately point to his spiritual experience as a solid justification of his *positive* beliefs, in the existence of God, the atoning efficacy of the Precious Blood, and so on : but I should dispute his right to use it as evidence for purely *negative* beliefs, as that there is no visible Church, or that the sacraments are not the normally necessary means of grace. The fact of his receiving grace is indisputable : but he cannot prove that this fact is not just as explicable on the basis of *Deus non alligatur mediis* as on the basis of *nulla sunt media ordinaria*.[2] The Salvationist's experience is good evidence, so far as it goes (and so, for that matter, is the experience of the non-Christian Theist, so far as *it* goes) : but I venture to submit that the Catholic's experience, which goes a long step further, is equally good evidence all the way.

I am thus prepared to admit that the Catholic system begins with experience and ends with experience : it

[1] As, for instance, by Prof. Kirsopp Lake in *The Earlier Epistles of St. Paul*.

[2] This phrase is a pseudo-scholastic coinage of my own.

rests, in the first instance, upon 'intuition', or the 'gift of Faith', and is verified by the consciousness of the reception of grace. But, again, it seems to me that this must necessarily be true of all Christianity, in whatever form it be held, and indeed of all Religion as such. If a religion could be discovered which could be fortified, so to speak, round the whole of its periphery with an absolutely complete system of objective and external guarantees, it would not be a religion, but a science.

VI

It is not unfair, I think, to claim that the form which these criticisms of yours have taken, together with the replies which I have made to them, illustrates in various ways and from various points of view the truth of what I said in my first letter, and repeated at the beginning of this, namely, that the difference between us is one of degree, and not of kind. It all turns upon the degree of closeness and exactness with which we conceive the Holy Spirit to have superintended the development of doctrine during the *second* stage of Revelation, that which (roughly speaking) began with Pentecost. And that again (I suggested) is determined by the degree of intensity in which we possess a certain fundamental intuition—the sense of the Spirit in the Church. I suppose that the conservative Modernist would say, from his point of view, that I had this sense in a somewhat exaggerated form—that I suffered, so to speak, from hyperaesthesia; and I suppose I should have to say, from my point of view, that *he* possessed it in a slightly atrophied form—though I should desire to guard myself, in the most explicit and emphatic manner possible, against the suspicion of even appearing to claim any spiritual or moral superiority on this ground. If the Traditionalist believes himself to have a somewhat clearer view of Divine truth than his Modernist brother, he would attribute his possession of this privilege solely to the mysterious predestination of God—οὐ τοῦ θέλοντος, οὐδὲ τοῦ τρέχοντος, ἀλλὰ τοῦ ἐλεοῦντος θεοῦ—and would never dream of claiming credit for himself or assuming an attitude of Pharisaical self-satisfaction.

However, this slight difference of intuition or assumption would not matter, if the Creeds and other utterances of Ecumenical authority contained none but propositions of the kind which you have designated *metaphysical*— that is, dealing with the being and attributes of God as He is in Himself. You say (p. 42) ' Where we propound to ourselves the same questions that are raised by the Creeds, especially so far as these questions relate to the metaphysical nature of the Godhead, my own belief is that they are rightly answered in the words of the Creeds ' ; and, if this language had been meant to apply to *all* the propositions in the Creeds, I should ask no more. If a man agrees with me in accepting all the deliveries of Ecumenical authority, I at least am not disposed (for practical purposes) to catechize him too closely as to his views about the inmost nature of that authority. If he believes that the Church has not actually erred, I should naturally refrain from raising the abstract question whether it might conceivably have erred. But I am afraid that this is not quite the case in the present instance. You draw a distinction between the *metaphysical* and the *historical* clauses of the Creeds—between those statements which relate to the interior life of the Godhead as it is in itself, and those which are concerned with the historical incarnate life of the Son of God upon earth. (I quite accept this distinction, which I had already drawn myself in thought. I refrained, indeed, from raising it in my first letter, in order to avoid what then seemed an unnecessary complication of the issue : but it is no longer possible to avoid its consideration, as our remaining differences hinge largely upon it.) And I understand you to contend that, whilst the degree of Divine guidance which you are willing to assume is sufficient to guarantee the (relative) truth of, or at any rate to lend a high degree of probability to, the 'metaphysical' propositions of the Creeds, it is not sufficient to afford a similar assurance in the case of some of the 'historical' propositions, if these are taken in their traditional sense, i.e. in that sense which has been attributed to them by the 'Church of the past'. These propositions are, I suppose, those which affirm the Virginal Conception and Birth of Christ, the *Descensus ad inferos*, the Resurrection, and the Ascension. You say that ' it is impossible that the dead hand of bygone generations should foreclose historical discussion at the present day '.

Now, before going any further, I feel compelled to dispute the cogency of the argument which you found upon the distinction between 'metaphysical' and 'historical' propositions. I see no reason in the nature of things why the Church should not have been Divinely guided as well in the selection of 'historical' as in that of 'metaphysical' propositions for embodiment in the Creeds. The old Greek philosopher says jestingly ' if you believe the poets when they tell you of the existence of the Gods, you must believe the poets when they tell you what the Gods are like '. In other words, it would seem *prima facie* that if you are going to trust religious authority at all, you must trust it all in all, as well in the sphere of history as in that of metaphysics—unless and until it makes some pronouncement which can be certainly shown to be untrue : in which case its supernatural claims are at once stripped from it, and it stands revealed as a pretence and a fraud. I know that you do not like the principle of 'all or nothing' as applied to matters of religious belief, and I am quite willing to confess that it has in the past been applied in a highly unwise and regrettable manner to matters which fall far short of fundamental importance—as, for instance, to the question of the truth of certain historical statements in the Old Testament : but when we come down to what is fundamental in the Christian Revelation (if we can ascertain it), we cannot assert the right to pick and choose without implicitly denying the idea of ' Revelation ' altogether. At any rate, *my* view of the authority of the Church (which, as I ventured to suggest just now, the criticisms contained in your last letter do not seem to me to have upset) forbids me to label some elements in the orthodox tradition ' certainly true ' and others ' doubtful ', or ' less certainly true ' ; and I should have thought that your vaguer, or less rigid, view would have applied equally to both categories of propositions. Even assuming your general position, I do not see what *a priori* ground there is for asserting that the distinction in respect to subject-matter (between ' metaphysical ' and ' historical ' propositions) necessarily involves a distinction in respect to certainty or validity. Why should we suppose that an ' historical ' proposition is more likely in the nature of things to be untrue than a ' metaphysical ' proposition ? Speaking of the ' metaphysical ' clauses, you say 'I fully believe that the ultimate formulations accepted by the Church were always in the right direction '—' I do not think there is one to which I should wish to offer anything that is of the nature of contradiction '—and so on ; and, so far as *a priori* considerations are concerned, I do not at present see why you should not (quite consistently with your own assumptions) repose in this position with regard to the ' historical ' clauses of the Creeds.

I do not, of course, forget that (whatever liberty the Continental Modernist may claim for himself in this matter) you at least only desire freedom ' to abstain from *full* affirmation of ' the clauses in question, not freedom to deny them, nor yet freedom to abstain altogether from any degree of affirmation of them. I should like to say that this position (although I do not share it) seems to me a perfectly clear and intelligible one, and I should not at all agree with those who find it over-subtle or hairsplitting. It seems, so far as I can gather, that it depends upon the application of the distinction between *form* and *content* which we have agreed to draw in respect of the 'metaphysical' clauses, to the historical clauses of the Creeds. For instance, in the case of the clauses 'Conceived of the Holy Ghost, born of the Virgin Mary' I understand you to maintain that the *content* consists in the general idea of a Supernatural Birth, a Birth which was more completely operated, permeated, and sanctified by the heavenly influences of the Holy Spirit than any other birth before or since: and that the *form* which has hitherto been worn by this idea is that of a Birth in which a human father had no share whatever. I suppose that you would draw a similar distinction in the case of the other three propositions enumerated above, viz. the *Descensus ad inferos*, the Resurrection, and the Ascension. And in all four cases, I gather, you would claim, whilst holding fast to what you have defined as the *content*, liberty to relax your grip upon the *form*, to the extent, at any rate, of 'abstaining from full affirmation'.

Perhaps I had better say at this point that in what follows I shall be no longer engaged in defending my own position—(that was stated in my first letter, and based upon 'intuition': and, as I have said, it seems to me, on the whole not to have been affected by the fire of criticism which you have directed upon it)—I propose in the rest of this paper to devote myself to attacking (of course in a genial spirit) your position.

I should in the first place challenge the legitimacy of the use which you make of the distinction between *form* and *content* in regard to the 'historical' clauses. In the case of the 'metaphysical' clauses, form and content are not merely *distinguishable*, but, so to speak, *detachable*. For instance, the content of the Homoousion clause—the general idea of Christ's Deity and Divine Sonship—was for a long time held in and by the Church apart from the actual thought-form of 'Identity of Substance' or 'Consubstantiality'. The content and the form were not, in the beginning, indissolubly soldered together : and I can quite well imagine a modern theologian claiming to detach the content from the form in which it has come down to us, and to hold the former whilst dropping, or relaxing his grip upon, the latter : and I should regard such a position as quite intelligible (though not, of course, consistent with perfect loyalty to Catholic teaching). But in the case of historical propositions in general—and, therefore, of the historical clauses of the Creeds in particular—I should contend that form and content are *distinguishable* only, and not *detachable*—like the concave and convex aspects of a mathematical curve. Take such an historical proposition as the following—' Charlotte Corday killed Marat.' Obviously here form and content exactly coincide, as in the case of a musical melody. They are certainly not detachable, and I am inclined to doubt whether they are really distinguishable. It follows, then, that an historical proposition must be either taken or left —and by ' taken ' I mean accepted, or assented to ; if it is only partially affirmed, it is really ' left '. Or, again, if only a modified form of it is accepted, it is really ' left ' ; e. g. if an historian were to tell me that he accepted the proposition instanced above in the sense that ' Charlotte Corday was indirectly instrumental in procuring Marat's death ', and still more if he were to interpret it as merely meaning that in the long run the spirit of freedom triumphs over tyranny, I should have to reply that he was not really accepting, but merely substituting another statement for, the statement proposed for his acceptance. I am therefore constrained to contend that the historical clauses of the Creeds cannot be placed in the same category as the metaphysical clauses : the distinction between form and content cannot usefully be applied to them : they are either eternally true, and to be taken, or eternally false, and to be left. There is no question of relative truth, of the Holy Spirit gently steering the tumultuous debates of contending theologians so as at last to educe the perfect form for the embodiment of a hitherto undefined content: the conception of a gradual fixation of what was once fluid, a progressive definition of what was once vague, cannot be applied to statements of plain historical fact, or what is alleged to be historical fact. The 'historical' clauses of the Creeds—*if they are true*—must thus represent an element of permanence, of immobility, of absence of development, existing side by side with the element of growth and efflorescence which manifests itself in the 'metaphysical' clauses. They are the solid, unchanging rock, above which the grove of 'metaphysical' dogmas grows and flourishes.

I do not, therefore, object to your describing the kind of continuity and identity, which I ascribe to the content of the 'historical' clauses, as a 'mechanical' identity, provided that the word 'mechanical' is not used as a question-begging epithet—i.e. provided that it is not assumed that what is 'mechanical' is somehow necessarily wrong or untrue. Nor have I any wish to quarrel with your simile of coins put into a box and taken out, absolutely unchanged, after the lapse of many years: I think it expresses quite admirably the kind of immobile sameness, of unchanging identity, which must necessarily be attributed to all *true* statements of historical fact, whether such statements occur in the Creeds or not.

All this may appear, at first sight, lamentably hard, and narrow, and rigid. But I would plead that after all it is simply common sense. An event happens: it happens in one way, and one only: having happened, it becomes part of the irrevocable past, and cannot be undone or altered or modified, even though some or many of its more direct consequences may be counteracted by human agency. A past event cannot grow, or develop, or evolve.

> μόνου γὰρ αὐτοῦ καὶ θεὸς στερίσκεται,
> ἀγένητα ποιεῖν ἄσσ' ἂν ᾖ πεπραγμένα.
> (Agathon, *ap.* Arist. *Eth. Nic.* vi. 2. 6.)

I am not sure that I should agree with the poet's limitations of the power of God in this regard; but certainly man cannot make that not to have happened which once has happened. No amount of research, of improvement of historical methods, of sharpening of analytic acumen, can *change* the past; we may discover that a historical proposition which we thought to be true was in reality false, but we cannot *make* a proposition which is objectively true to be false, or vice versa. Consequently, true propositions about the past must necessarily be immobile and unchanging : the proposition, 'Julius Caesar was murdered by Brutus, Cassius, and their friends,' was as true on March 16, 44 B. C. as it is to-day, November 20, A. D. 1915 ; nor has there been a single moment of time between these two points when it has not been true. The lapse of time has neither added to, nor taken away from, its unchanging truth : nor will it be any less, or any more, true than it is to-day on November 20, A. D. 3015 or 5015. Similarly the proposition, 'Alexander the Great was the son of Zeus and Olympias,' is, and always has been from the first moment of its formulation, and to the end of time always will be, completely false.

Of course, a great many philosophical subtleties have been raised, especially in recent thought, with regard to the conception of ' fact ' in history : and if we were engaged in a merely *eristic* controversy, you could doubtless make great play with them. But, as we are trying in a friendly spirit to hammer out the truth, I imagine that you will raise no objection to my use of the words ' fact ', ' true ', and ' false ' in the plain man's sense, without further refinements or definitions.

The general conclusion which seems to result from the foregoing remarks may be expressed as follows : the distinction between form and content in respect of the historical clauses is a distinction in thought only : in reality, the form and the content of these clauses are inseparable and indeed coincident. They are therefore either true as they stand or false as they stand: and the possibility of 'partial affirmation' seems to be excluded. I imagine that you would admit this in the case of some at least of the historical clauses, viz. those which affirm that our Lord died by crucifixion. The clause, 'Crucifixus etiam pro nobis: sub Pontio Pilato passus et sepultus est,' contains (should we not both agree?) a plain statement of (alleged) historical fact, which must either be taken or left. There is no possibility of detaching 'content' from 'form', and holding the one whilst dropping the other. If a modern theologian, as the result of his anthropological studies, were to conclude that the whole account of the Crucifixion is a form of the 'Rex Nemorensis' story and that the historical Jesus really lived to a ripe old age and died a natural death, we should both surely say, 'Well, that is your opinion, and (as this is a free country) you have a perfect right to hold it: but I am afraid that I cannot admit that you are a Christian, or that you can honestly repeat those clauses of the Creeds, which affirm the Crucifixion, in any sense whatever.' To adopt any other attitude would be to dissolve historical Christianity into a pleasing mirage, a picturesque illusion, which might be useful as a political instrument for keeping the masses in order, but could never command the allegiance of educated men.

VII

At this point I can imagine the 'conservative Modernist' interjecting, 'This is all very well: but it is all written from an *a priori* point of view, which may well be as deceptive as many *a priori* arguments have proved to be in the past. Look at the question for a moment simply in the light of the present religious and scientific situation. On the one hand, we *can't* simply affirm the "historical", or rather the "historical *and* miraculous" clauses, simply as they stand: "imperious necessity", or "what some of us think imperious necessity" (p. 8) compels us to "loosen our hold upon" the belief in the Virgin Birth: "we are convinced that bodies" in New Testament times "did not float in the air or materialize and dematerialize at will" (p. 16), and therefore we cannot accept the ideas of the Resurrection and the Ascension in exactly that form in which the early Church held them: we do not imagine that the spirits of the departed are confined in a hollow cavern under the ground, and we cannot therefore take the *Descensus ad inferos* in its literal sense. On the one hand, we neither can nor will give up the Christian Faith *in toto*, as you would apparently have us do. We cannot repudiate our deepest spiritual experience at the dictates of a cold and relentless logic. There is therefore nothing else for it. We cannot accept these things in their literal sense, but we must accept them in *some* sense, so as not to forfeit continuity with the past. We are compelled by facts to find some way of holding the general ideas which lie behind these clauses, whilst dropping the literal sense: whether the distinction of "form" and "content" be applicable or not, some such distinction—the exact verbal phrase matters comparatively little—is a practical necessity.'

VIII

My comments upon this series of contentions can, I think, be compressed within a brief compass.

(1) You will notice that this argument, as I have ventured to formulate it, speaks of 'the "historical", *or rather the*" *historical* and *miraculous*", clauses'.[1] I am

---

[1] Of course, 'miraculous clauses' is a compendious expression for 'clauses which affirm miracles'.

emboldened to express the contention in this way by the fact that (as I have assumed) you have no objection to the acceptance of the Crucifixion-clause (which is certainly 'historical' and not 'metaphysical'), in its plain and literal sense—in the same sense in which it was accepted four hundred, eight hundred, sixteen hundred years ago. But if I am right in this, a consequence of the utmost importance results. It would seem that you object to these four clauses precisely because they affirm *miracles* —not because they are affirmations about events in past time. In other words, your attitude on this subject is determined by what I must be pardoned for calling antimiraculous presuppositions. And at this point I fear we decisively part company. Take such a sentence as this : ' We ' (that is, presumably, ' conservative Modernists ') ' are convinced that bodies in [New Testament] days did not float in the air or materialize and dematerialize at will.' By this I imagine you mean that you are convinced that bodies *could* not have floated—that it was *a priori* and inherently impossible for them to float in the air ; for it would be obviously impossible to demonstrate *a posteriori*, by an exhaustive record of the movements of all bodies during ' New Testament times ', that none of them actually did perform this feat. We have therefore to do with an *a priori* assumption, of the impossibility of bodies floating in the air. Now I am afraid I must say (*a*) that I am equally firmly convinced that God has the power, and might well have the will, to levitate bodies, whether in ' New Testament ' or in more recent times : in other words, that I do believe in the abstract possibility of such levitations : and (*b*) that I think there is good *a posteriori* evidence for the occurrence of such events, not only in the first century, but in every succeeding century down to the present day. From the standpoint of *my* assumptions, I see no reason to doubt the reality of these phenomena, not only in the case of New Testament personages, but also in those of (e.g.) St. Francis of Assisi and St. Gerard Majella. So on this point I fear that we are hopelessly divided. I suppose the same thing applies to the clauses affirming the Miraculous Conception and Birth. You think that 'imperious necessity' forbids you to accept these clauses in their plain and ordinary sense—in other words, you feel it to be *a priori* impossible, or at any rate highly improbable, that Jesus Christ was really born of the body of a maiden, without the agency of a human father: I have no such feeling, and am absolutely unconscious of the existence of any such 'imperious necessity'. For me, the supposition that Joseph was somehow enabled to beget a child who was the Almighty Word of God is *a priori* just as improbable as—I am inclined to think, rather more improbable than—the supposition that the Word of God was born as the child of a Virgin Mother. And here, it seems to me, we have laid bare another difference of fundamental assumption, of equal importance with that which I have already discussed in the first part of this paper. The question of exact extent to which the Holy Spirit controlled the development of ('metaphysical') doctrine—and the question of the abstract or *a priori* possibility of certain miracles—those are the real points at issue. I have tried to set down what I think on the first of these questions, and I will not go over that ground again. As for the second, I do not wish to trench upon the ground of your discussion with the Dean, and I will therefore content myself with noting its existence: though I cannot forbear from observing that I have yet to learn what logical criterion you employ for discerning miracles which you are willing to accept (miracles which you call *supra naturam*) from those which 'imperious necessity' forbids you to accept (the class described as *contra naturam*). Until some definition of the terms '*supra*', '*contra*', and '*natura*' is produced, this distinction must inevitably wear some appearance of arbitrariness. But these questions belong to your other symposium, and I must resist the temptation to pursue them further.

(2) 'But', you may say, 'what about the other argument against the literal acceptation of the "historical and miraculous clauses"—the contention that two of them, at least, presuppose a conception of the physical universe which no sane man of modern times can possibly hold? Even supposing that we agree to differ about the abstract possibility of such events as the Virginal Birth and the Resurrection, is it not clear that the clause affirming the *Descensus ad inferos*, taken in the sense in which it was understood by its first formulators, presupposes the idea of a Sheol or Hades locally situated beneath the earth—and that the clause affirming the Ascension, in the mind of the primitive Church, assumed the idea of a geographical Heaven locally situated above the vault of the sky? If this is so, it follows that even the most rigidly orthodox of modern theologians does not, and cannot (without raising doubts as to his sanity), accept the ideas of the *Descensus* and the Ascension in the same sense as that in which they were accepted by the primitive Church: and that at once disposes of the "unalterability" which you attribute to the "historical" clauses of the Creeds. If these two clauses *cannot* be accepted in the same sense in which they were accepted fourteen hundred years ago, it is obvious that the other two need not. In the case of the *Descensus* and the Ascension, the distinction between the permanent ideaf content and the temporary and transitory form or husk is forced upon us by the facts; and if this method of interpretation is necessary in the case of the *Descensus* and the Ascension, it must be at least permissible in the case of the Virginal birth and of the Resurrection.'

I should reply to this contention by disputing the truth of what is apparently its major premiss—viz. the assertion that the primitive Catholic Church, in defining the *Descensus* and Ascension as parts of the essential

Deposit of Faith, meant to commit itself, and did commit itself, to the hypotheses of a local and geographical Heaven and Hades. As I have formulated it, this assertion seems to me both unproved and unprovable. It is doubtless quite possible—it may be probable—that many, or most, primitive Christians did as a matter of fact believe in the geocentric theory of the universe, and thought of Heaven as a place locally situated above their heads, and Hades, or Limbo, as locally situated beneath their feet : but he who would infer from this that *the Church, as such,* believed in and meant to teach a geographical Heaven and Hell would seem to lay himself open to the charge of committing the ' Fallacy of Composition ' in a somewhat obvious form. So far as I can see, the Church, as distinct from individual Fathers and theologians, always meant by the *Descensus*, Resurrection, and Ascension exactly what an educated modern Catholic means by them now, namely (a) that our Lord, during the time which elapsed between His Death on the Cross and His Resurrection, vouchsafed to dwell, in respect of His Sacred Humanity, as a disembodied human spirit, in the ' place ', or ' state ', or ' sphere ' (human language is necessarily imperfect) of departed human spirits ; that His human experience included, not only the actual suffering of death, but the experience of what comes after death :

(b) that on the third day after His death, He returned in His disembodied human spirit, from the world of the dead, and took active possession once more of the Body which had meanwhile been lying in Joseph's new tomb : that, clothed in this risen Body, He sojourned with His Apostles, and instructed them in the things pertaining to the kingdom of God ; and

(c) that after some time spent in this mysterious risen life, He entered upon a condition of supreme glory and power in the spiritual world, and definitely departed, so far as His visible and physical presence was concerned,

88 *Form and Content in Christian Tradition*

out of the plane of the material world—a spiritual event which was sacramentally imaged forth in the sphere of sense by the rising of His body in the air, before the eyes of His adherents, until it was veiled from sight by a cloud. No one will contend that primitive Christians meant less than this by the *Descensus*, Resurrection, and Ascension : and I know of no evidence that the primitive Church, *as such*, meant more.

IX

It will now be clear what reply I should return to the argument which you briefly develop on pp. 49, 50. You say, 'the New Testament supplies the *data* which are worked up in the Creeds. It follows that, if there is a progressive reinterpretation of the one, the same thing must hold good of the other.' I may perhaps be permitted to expand this argument as follows : ' The Creeds are summaries of doctrine collected out of Scripture, and have no independent authority of their own ; any reinterpretation therefore of Scripture, the fundamental authority, must involve a reinterpretation of the Creeds, which only possess a derived authority.' I must point out that the position from which this argument starts is one which those who think with me would entirely repudiate. We do not believe that the Creeds are merely summaries of, and dependent upon, Scripture. Historically, the old Roman baptismal Creed (if Dr. Burn is to be trusted), which was the germ of our present ' Apostles' Creed ', is actually prior to the formation of a New Testament Canon ; it is certain at any rate that the baptismal (and, later, the conciliar) Creeds, the Canon of the New Testament, and the three-fold ministry developed side by side in the Church from the second century onwards, and I need not remind you that the New Testament Canon was not definitively closed until the Quini-Sextine Council, three hundred years after the formulation of the Nicene and Niceno-Constantinopolitan Symbols. Creed, Canon of Scripture, hierarchy—these (I should contend) are the triple outgrowth of the fundamental Deposit of Faith, as it developed and fructified under the inspiration of the Holy Spirit. The relation between Scripture and Creed is thus collateral, not one of direct dependence or descent. Both alike are embodiments of the Deposit of fundamental ideas; the one pictures the Deposit as it was within forty or fifty years of its promulgation, the other represents it as it was after three, four, and five centuries of development had passed over it; the one contains the Deposit, still fluid and undefined on its 'metaphysical' side, in a collection of miscellaneous documents, no one containing the whole, but each illustrating an aspect, or aspects—the other enshrines it in clear-cut and finished phrases, each standing for a technical conceptual form. The New Testament is, so to speak, a sort of composite photograph of the Church and Faith—the total fact of Christianity—as they were in their infancy: and we appeal to the New Testament in support of the Creeds, *not* to prove them to ourselves (for they are already sufficiently guaranteed by our fundamental postulate of the infallibility of the Church) but to prove them to outsiders. The New Testament (on the Catholic view) is, like the photograph which a traveller carries in his passport, for purposes of identification; he does not carry the picture of himself as he was in order to prove his own identity to himself, but in order to prove it to others—customs and military officials. So the Church, wherever she goes, carries about with her the New Testament, in order to prove to the inquiring outsider that she, the Church of the twentieth century, of London, Paris, and New York, is, in essence, the same Church, teaching the same Faith, as the Church of the first century, of Jerusalem, Antioch, and Ephesus.

The above is the sketchiest possible treatment of

a great subject; but I hope enough has been said to indicate the main reason why your argument based upon the alleged dependence of the Creeds upon Scripture has no cogency for us. Of course, I should not in any case admit that it is necessary to impose a symbolic reinterpretation upon the parts of Scripture which deal with the four clauses in question. As I have said elsewhere, I cannot, with the best will in the world, rid myself of the impression that all, or at any rate most, of the destructive criticism of these passages is, if closely and candidly analysed, based upon *a priori* considerations; that it all starts, in reality if not in appearance, from the unexpressed assumption that God either could not or would not have worked such wonders as the Virginal Conception and the Resurrection as ordinarily understood. I trust that I am not insensible to the effect of genuine *a posteriori* evidence: and *if* at any future time an ostrakon or a papyrus leaf is unearthed at Nazareth which proves beyond the shadow of a doubt that Jesus was the son of Joseph, I shall be prepared to take the consequences. I shall frankly admit that Catholic Christianity has tumbled down with a crash, and I shall proceed to look round for some other theory of the universe. But I have a shrewd suspicion that no such ostrakon or papyrus ever will emerge.

X

I am afraid that this letter has grown to an inordinate length. But you will readily understand that loyalty to my own position forbade me to leave any of your points unanswered. And a satisfactory commentary must necessarily be rather longer than the text upon which it is based. May I, in conclusion, sum up in a few words the stage which our argument seems to me to have reached?

1. We both agree to distinguish between the 'metaphysical' and the 'historical' clauses of the Creeds.

[By 'Creeds' I presume we both mean all documents possessing Ecumenical authority.]
2. In respect of the 'metaphysical' clauses we agree to distinguish between 'form' and 'content'.
3. We agree, further, that the 'content', at least, of these clauses is *per se* unalterable, inasmuch as it comes to us by Revelation from God.
4. As to the 'form', *I* maintain that it is *per accidens* unalterable : that, although a particular content may not always have been associated with a particular form, nevertheless, now that the association has been set up by Church authority, it is not open to individual believers to dissolve it ;

You, on the other hand, are not prepared to commit yourself even to a *per accidens* unalterability of the 'form '—but you say that, as a matter of fact, you have no desire to alter it. So that on this point, although we diverge in theory, we appear to agree in practice.
5. When, however, we come to consider the 'historical' clauses, a much greater divergence appears. In respect of these clauses, *you* maintain that 'form' and 'content' are not only distinguishable but also separable, and you desire to retain the latter whilst dropping, or not firmly holding, the former ;

I, on the other hand, maintain that in these clauses, as in all (alleged) plain statements of historical fact, 'form' and 'content' are absolutely coincident, and that these clauses must therefore be either taken or left : and, of course, my fundamental conviction of the inerrancy of orthodox Christian tradition compels me to 'take' them.
6. The slight divergence of view noted under (4) and the considerable divergence noted under (5), are both ultimately traceable to a difference in respect of fundamental, unproved, and unprovable assumptions or axioms—to a difference in respect of ἀρχαὶ

ἀναπόδεικτοι. I start from the assumption of the infallibility of the Church, and the *a priori* possibility of certain miracles : *you* start from the assumption of a providential guidance of the Church which does not amount to 'infallibility', and of the *a priori* impossibility, or at any rate extreme improbability, of these miracles.

7. I quite admit that my ἀρχαί are ἀναπόδεικτοι— reached by intuition and not by ratiocination : but I contend (*a*) that *any* ἀρχαί, especially in religious matters, must necessarily be indemonstrable; (*b*) and that yours are just as much so as mine.

And there, for the present, I must leave it. In a general sense, I still think that the difference between us is one of degree, not of kind. So far as I can see, your position is not exactly a 'New Theology'; it is in essence the Old Theology, only with a large bite taken out of it. And this fact seems to hold out considerable hopes of eventual agreement, if not between you and me, at any rate between those who think with you and those who think with me. But it has another consequence which I feel bound to explain. Precisely because it is, not an entirely new position, but (as I should hold) a somewhat mutilated form of the old position, it seems to me entirely destitute of the 'enormous strength' which you claim for it in your first paper. The old position in its entirety, given the fundamental assumption of the 'infallibility' of the Church, *does* seem to me to be 'enormously strong', and to be proof against all assaults ; and such an entirely new position as that of Professor Troeltsch, which has little, if anything, in common with historical Christianity, also seems to me to be 'enormously strong'. If I may develop the metaphor from trench warfare, hinted at in your first paper (p. 7), it seems to me that there are two possible policies. There is the policy of doggedly holding the old line of fortifications as it has always stood, with a full recognition of the fact that a breach in the line means encirclement and destruction : this is the policy of Traditionalism. There is also the policy of evacuating the old line altogether, and withdrawing to a new and self-contained set of trenches further up the hill : this would be the policy of Troeltsch. But your policy appears to be that of surrendering three or four ' traverses ' to the enemy, and yet endeavouring to hold the rest of the line—a policy which exposes you at once to an enfilading fire, and (it seems to me) must sooner or later involve withdrawal altogether, or else encirclement. Of course, the practical course which I should wish to advocate would be, not retirement to the new line, but reoccupation of the temporarily abandoned ' traverses '.

In any case, permit me to apologize for the length of this letter, and believe me to be,

Very sincerely yours,
N. P. WILLIAMS.

DR. SANDAY'S REJOINDER.

My dear Williams,

I am glad that you have given yourself full scope for your reply. The result, I must needs think, will be equally satisfactory on both sides of our argument. Those who agree with you will see in your letter an unusually frank and clear statement of the logical structure of their own position; and those who agree with me will have the advantage of knowing, better (if I am not mistaken) than they have ever known before, precisely what they have to reckon with.

You have been specially successful, if I may be allowed to say so, in striking a balance between our opposing views, in bringing out the extent of our agreement and showing precisely at what point we begin to part company. I do not think that I have ever been engaged in a controversy in which I felt this so strongly. From this point of view, I could be well content to leave our discussion where it now stands. At the same time some new points have come up, or at least present themselves with somewhat greater insistence. These points perhaps still need a little further elucidation, which I will now try to offer. When that has been done—so far at least as I am concerned—our discussion may close.

I

The summaries that you give from time to time are all that I could wish. It has only sometimes happened that, in paraphrasing an argument or opinion of mine, you have fallen into language which I could not altogether endorse; you have stated your point in a way that is natural to yourself, but not quite equally natural to me.

This has happened specially in contexts in which you are appealing to authority. Authority plays a rather different part in your scheme of beliefs and in mine. For me, the ultimate standard of judgement is what I conceive to be truth. Authority has its weight; but I could not accept a thing purely upon authority, if I did not also believe it to be true. With me, the idea of truth stands behind everything else; with you, if I am not mistaken, the idea of authority sometimes takes precedence and becomes a ground of acceptance independently of truth. I might perhaps put it that, with you, certain propositions are 'true because taught', whereas with me they would be 'taught because true'.

It may perhaps be worth while to state explicitly that, whereas there are many different degrees of truth and sincerity, the modernist (as I understand Modernism) aims before all things at the highest kind of both; he does not think that he has attained to the highest truth or the highest sincerity until he can speak from personal conviction. He may recognize degrees short of this, and acquiesce in them provisionally; but he always feels that his acquiescence is provisional; he has not yet attained to the *vérité vraie*, which is the crowning stage of all.

I do not mention this because I think that anything of great importance in our present discussion turns upon it. I do not remember that anything is involved that goes beyond the question of wording. But, for complete mutual understanding, it is perhaps as well to be quite explicit.

I altogether welcome the general conclusion to which you come that the differences between us are differences of degree rather than of kind. You more than once express pleasure and to some extent surprise at finding that this is so (pp. 24, 36, 55, 56; cf. 71, 92, *supra*). And I should myself be inclined to say that, if our discussion had no other effect than to bring out this, it would not have been in vain.

The points between us that appear still to need a little further elucidation are these:

(1) The different footing of what we agree to call the metaphysical and historical clauses of the Creed.

(2) In connexion with this some further remarks should be made on the subject of Miracle.
(3) The degree of enlightenment conferred upon the Church by the operation of the Holy Spirit.
(4) The validity of the assumption on which your view of this enlightenment rests.

To complete the survey there should be added

(5) some further consideration of the positive grounds on which a reasoned view of this subject rests; and lastly,
(6) an attempt to indicate more precisely the place of Relativity of Expression in the whole scheme.

It really is a connected and coherent scheme which I desire to put forward; and by it I am prepared either to stand or fall.

II

When I drew a distinction between the metaphysical and historical clauses of the Creeds and expressed my intention of confining my claim for latitude of interpretation to the latter, I did not intend to do this on the ground of any inherent difference between the two sets of clauses in the nature of things. I do, as a matter of fact, believe that there is an element of relativity in all human expression, and therefore in both classes alike. The same kind of relativity is really apparent in each class: relativity to the general structure of the human mind and to the particular phase of its history to which the clauses of the Creeds and the statements which they embody belong.

It is only in practice that a difference of treatment becomes desirable. In my original paper (p. 12, *supra*) I expressed the view that the ancients showed a tendency to over-definition and that in modern times the demand for such definition had become less than it was. I do not deny that, if the right of criticism is pressed, it may be necessary to examine closely the history and special application of every metaphysical term that is used. But at the same time I bear in mind, what you have yourself pointed out, the essential simplicity of these terms; and, beyond a general caution against over-refinement, I do not find myself called upon to criticize. It might be otherwise, if there were any generally accepted philosophical system current to-day and not current in the early centuries of the Christian Era. If there had been such a system, it might be necessary to draw up a scheme of equivalents and to translate the language of the past into that of the present. But, in default of any such generally accepted system, the necessity does not arise. We are content to make the best use of the old language that we can.

But this state of things does not hold good in the region of history. History is more distinctly a progressive science than philosophy. There is a greater amount of general agreement as to the nature of the progress made and as to the methods now in use as compared with those employed in the past. The full application of criticism to history is a product of comparatively modern times. We should not I suppose be far wrong if we were to regard it as characteristic—and increasingly characteristic—of the last hundred and fifty years.

When I was a boy, we happened to have at home a translation of the *Histoire Ancienne* of Charles Rollin (1661–1741), which had a considerable vogue in its day. I remember well how much I enjoyed the story of Cyrus, King of Persia, as told by this writer. It was only many years later that I discovered that this version of the story was based upon Xenophon's *Cyropaedia*, which is now known to be largely romance. That is just an example of the difference between the way in which history was written some two hundred years ago and the way in which it is written now. Naturally, allowance has to be made for this difference. Within the last hundred years a complete revolution in the art of writing history has taken place. And nowhere has this revolution been more

98 *Form and Content in Christian Tradition*

marked than in the portion of history covered by the Bible. The change of treatment came in first for the period included in the Old Testament; it is only by degrees that it has been carried forward to the period included in the New.

It is true that it would still be premature to speak of an accepted version of New Testament history; but we may, within limits, speak of a version that would find very wide acceptance of the history embraced by the Old Testament. We are compelled to look ahead; and I confess that I do not think it too soon to let our general view of the New Testament be affected by our general view of the Old. It seems to me that this revision involves a revised conception of many of the events recorded in both the Testaments. We begin with the Old Testament; but I am very sure that it is quite impossible to begin and end there. I have no doubt in my own mind that the process begun in reference to the Old Testament must be carried forward to the New.

The further consequence follows that, if the New Testament is affected, the Creeds must also be affected. By that of course I do not mean the wording of the Creeds, but the meaning that we attach to the words. It is here that you and I diverge. I know that you regard the Creeds as possessing an independent authority in themselves apart from the New Testament. I can grant you that those by whom they were composed had access to a rather wider literature than is contained within the Canon. For instance, they had some Apocryphal Gospels which have now been lost; and they had also (at the time of the composition of the nucleus of the Old Roman Creed, which is the basis of our Apostles' Creed) a certain amount of oral tradition, which was rapidly running dry. But you would hardly say that this additional literature and additional tradition contributed anything substantial to what we still know from the New Testament. You would hardly say that the Descent into Hades (which was of course a later insertion in the Apostles' Creed) or the Ascension meant for the authors of the Creed anything different from what they meant for the New Testament writers.

The modern historian is obliged to go behind both the New Testament records and the Creeds. He asks himself what really happened; and then he finds that he has to discount somewhat the tradition as it has come down to him. You yourself do this to a certain extent (p. 87), and I go rather further; that is the difference between us.

III

At this point comes in the question of Miracles. I naturally cannot attempt, and it is not necessary that I should attempt, to go into the whole of this question. But it may not be inappropriate for me to try to state my view of the position in which the controversy seems at the present time to stand.

1. I have never said, and never thought, that miracles are impossible. If we take miracle in the sense of 'wonder' —an event outside the common order, and specially connected with some great spiritual manifestation emerging from that order—then, I am quite prepared to say that there have been many well-attested miracles, which have played a real and important part in the history of the Christian religion.

It is only quite a small group of alleged miracles that I feel called upon to challenge, and only a particular aspect even of them. It was really in order to narrow the ground to the consideration of this small group, that I suggested the distinction between miracles *supra naturam* and *contra naturam*. My object was not scientific but practical. I thought that the distinction would convey a sufficiently clear meaning to ordinary people. By 'nature' I meant what are commonly called 'the laws of matter and motion'. I was willing to admit every form of miracle that was consistent with the recognition of these laws. I was quite prepared for the presence in the universe of extraordinary forces, expressing themselves in extraordinary phenomena. I do not doubt at all that the public ministry of our Lord and of the Apostles was accompanied by such phenomena. By the term *supra naturam* I intended to recognize their extraordinary character; I intended to mark them as the fitting sign or effect of a Cause or Causes higher than the ordinary. We have sufficient warrant for believing that from time to time such causes have been at work in the world; and we regard them as culminating in the activities of our Lord Jesus Christ and those whom He chose to continue and carry on His mission.

But the well-attested wonders that may be regarded as coming under this description have all had analogies of some kind in the ordinary course of nature; they have been in harmonious relation to that course; they have never required a breach or contradiction of the natural order. It is precisely here that we draw the line. Even the alleged events that really imply such a breach or contradiction are very few in number. They are so few as to raise grave doubts whether they can be regarded as strictly historical.

2. As a matter of fact, it is becoming increasingly difficult for the modern mind to give full credence to stories of this nature. That is the position of things with which we have to deal. There is a reluctance to believe, a sense of incongruity, a difficulty in harmonizing all the details of these events with the regular course of the universe as we see it.

I have myself tried to analyse this widespread unwillingness to believe, and to trace it to its roots. But my attempt has been criticized. The Dean of Christ Church thinks that I exaggerate the stringency of the belief in the uniformity of nature. Dr. A. C. Headlam regards me as involved in the methods and presuppositions of mid-

Victorian physics. It may be true that I approached the subject from a standpoint that may be described as mid-Victorian. I was not ignorant of the change that has come over the modern scientific conception of matter. But, so far as I could judge, it did not seem to me that this change had made any difference to the essential balance of the argument. I do not think it can be said that the belief in the strict uniformity of nature is less strong than it was. I take that belief as marking a deep-rooted element in the constitution of nature as God has willed it. Indeed, the evidence for this kind of regularity is so overwhelming that I cannot help regarding the will that finds expression in it as deeply rooted in the character of God Himself. For this reason I myself share in the *praeiudicium* or reluctance to accept anything inconsistent with it of which I have spoken. Given two hypotheses for explaining a particular narrative, that which does not involve any breach of the regular order has for me a strong presumption in its favour. I always bear in mind the possibility that a momentous act like the Incarnation might well be supposed to have been attended by special circumstances. But the special circumstances alleged seem upon the face of them far more likely to have been produced by a transitory phase in man's ideas about God than by a real exception in the mode of operation of God Himself.

3. I speak of this as an antecedent presumption. But so far as I am myself concerned, the really determining trains of argument have come from the side of history and criticism or from that of psychology. Two such processes of reasoning had been at work in my mind. On the one hand, there was the approach to the New Testament through the Old. On the other hand, there was the direct study of the New Testament itself. These processes converged upon the same result. If we isolated that particular aspect of miracle which seemed to raise the greatest difficulties, within this limited sphere,

just the worst of those difficulties seemed to dissolve away.

There are, it is well known, certain narratives of miracle in the Old Testament, clustering especially round two events or groups of events, the Exodus of Israel from Egypt with the Wanderings in the Desert, and the activity of the prophets Elijah and Elisha. But in each of these cases there was room for the application of criticism. In regard to the Exodus and Wanderings, there was an interval that would have to be measured by centuries between the events and the earliest record. In the narratives of Elijah and Elisha, the interval was not so great as this ; but still there was a substantial interval, a space of time quite long enough to allow for the growth of legend. A closer examination seemed to show that, while there was a nucleus of history, there was an outside fringe of folk-lore the details of which were filled in by the popular imagination. In no single instance, throughout the whole of the Old Testament, was there such authentic first-hand testimony as could establish the presence of details which involved any real contradiction of the laws of nature. Not only was there always time for the accretion of such details, but in several of the more noteworthy examples it seemed easy to see how they might have arisen.

But if this general result of Old Testament criticism held good, there remained only the miracles of the New Testament. And these again fell into two classes, those which did imply and those which did not imply any real contradiction of natural laws. And there was further to be observed a remarkable coincidence between this distinction as to the nature of the miracles and a parallel distinction as to the nature of the evidence on which the accounts of them rested. The first-class evidence, that of St. Paul's Epistles, was available only for the miracles of the first order. Nowhere did this first-class testimony extend to and cover the kind of details that were peculiar to the miracles of the second order. In other words, the evidence for this smaller class of details everywhere broke down; there might be evidence enough to establish the general truth of the event to which it referred, but when it came to be applied to details—and especially to these more questionable details—the evidence always proved to be insufficient.

While this result seemed to emerge in the regular course of documentary criticism, it was met and confirmed by another result which seemed to come out upon the side of history. Whenever suspicious details are found in our documents, the next question that has to be asked is, how did they come there? If they are not inherent in the facts, the probability will be that they came in through the process of transmission—that they came in through the play of the popular imagination upon the facts. The critic has then to seek for the kind of stimuli that would naturally suggest such accretions. He is not always called upon to do this; but it strengthens his case when he is able to do it. And it is not incumbent upon him to lay his finger upon the precise cause which led to any particular effect. It will be as much as can be reasonably expected if he is able to point to some generic tendency which might naturally give rise to the particular effect that has to be accounted for.

It seems to me that not only a *vera causa* but a sufficient cause for what we conceive to be adventitious details in the Gospel narratives is supplied by a single broadly operative cause, which may be described as the psychology of the chain of witnesses and writers. The writer is the last link in the chain; and he sets down what is in his mind. But this content of his mind is the final resultant of a process at several points in which there has been a play of influences, more often unconscious than conscious, which have gone to shape the form of the written narrative as it ultimately appears. Among these shaping influences, I strongly suspect that one of the most important has been that derived from precedents and analogies supplied by the Old Testament. In any case, the minds of the successive witnesses and writers were full of these precedents and analogies; and, without knowing it, first one and then another contributed a detail here and a detail there which made up the total presentment of the picture as we have it.

In due course it will be incumbent on scholars to plot out a rough draft, susceptible of improvement and gradually improved, of this reconstructed process as they conceive of it. They start from the written document, but work their way backwards as well as they can to something approximately representing the original facts so far as they can guess at them. The result must needs be precarious; no one will ever be able to say 'This is what really happened'; the most that can be done will be to sketch something like what we may believe to have happened. But one tentative sketch may be more like than another; the success of the synthesis will correspond to the success of the analysis. God will accept what is offered to Him in an honest and true heart according to the best of such powers as His servants can dedicate to Him.

IV

That is what I may call the modernist's ideal. It is modest, but it is quite sincere; and it will have at least the advantage of being all of a piece with any other studies in which he may be engaged. If his proper province is history, he will not have one measure for sacred history and another for profane. There will be no close compartments. He will move backwards and forwards from the one ground to the other with ease and freedom.

You and I are both sensitive as to the relation in which we stand to the great movements of thought which are outside although they may include us. But we are sensitive in different directions and with reference to different movements. You desire to subordinate yourself to the great body of Catholic opinion. I should be sorry to lose touch with this; but at the same time its hold upon me is secondary, rather than primary. I should be even more sorry to lose touch with what I may call the world of science. I profoundly believe that in neither direction is any such sacrifice required of me. I profoundly believe that a presentation of Christianity is possible which shall be at once in strict and full continuity with the past and shall yet be in complete harmony with the most assured results of progressive science in the present—with progressive science on all its sides, not only physiological and biological but historical, exegetical, and (in a sound and sober sense) critical. All that I need to cement this far-reaching harmony is a due allowance for what I have called 'the difference of times' in the earlier statements of the Christian creed as compared with the revised statement in which we take it to ourselves to-day. I know that you challenge the phrase; and I know that it is challenged by those whom you would claim as friends and allies. But my contention is that the phrase represents an absolutely certain fact which, whether it is challenged or not, cannot be avoided, but must before long come to be recognized as a truism. Every age has its own complete circle of ideas; and any single section of those ideas stands in relation to all the rest, and must inevitably change as they change. As well bid the stream stop running, or the tree and the plant stop growing, as attempt to arrest and petrify the normal progressive movements of the human mind.

Yet I perfectly admit that this solidarity in movement —like the steady, irresistible advance of a glacier which

> moveth all together if it move at all—

is only one-half of the truth. The other half is the idea of fixity, stability, and permanence. In nature we see a balance between these two great principles. And I do not doubt that there is a like balance in the world of thought and belief. My endeavour is to maintain an equilibrium between the two sides. I would fain think that I do this more consistently and satisfactorily than you do. It seems to me that, on your view, the balance inclines too much on the side of permanence as compared with that of change. All turns on those two unfortunate expressions, 'infallibility' and 'unalterability',[1] which you are so loth to let go. Both seem to me to conflict with the analogy of nature. No such thing as a real and strict infallibility exists here below; and no such thing as real exemption from the law of flux and change can be verified in human experience.

You seek to establish the idea of fixity by an appeal to the comforting sense of security which it gives to those who hold it. You describe yourself as floating along a broad stream, the stream of orthodox Christian tradition or Catholic Christianity. You surrender yourself wholly to this stream, and you speak of the comfort which such surrender brings. Whenever I come across this argument from the comfortableness of the Catholic system, I am always reminded of that famous saying of Dr. Johnson's about the Church of Rome: 'I would be a Papist if I could; I have fear enough; but an obstinate rationality prevents me.' The Church of Rome has its attractive features, especially certain types of saintliness; but much that might be a temptation to others is no temptation to me—for the reason alleged by Dr. Johnson.

I doubt if it is good for us to be too comfortable. It is more bracing to feel that one stands foursquare to all the winds that blow. And other sources may be found for the exhilarating sense of being borne upon the breast of buoyant waters.

No Christian need be devoid of the feeling of comfort.

---

[1] The weakened sense which you attach to these terms on pp. 23, 33, 67 goes far to meet me. But I should have thought that it was better to give up the words altogether.

And I would submit that that feeling owes more to that which is common to all forms of Christianity than it does to the distinctive tenets of Catholicism—not to speak of the uncertainty whether the assumptions on which those tenets rest are well founded.

However, I do not forget that the cleavage between us on this head may easily be exaggerated. I too believe, as you believe, that the Church of Christ has been divinely guided in its definitions of doctrine. It is only that I cannot go with you in thinking that these definitions shut out all possibility of change. I am content to leave them as they are in their essential content; I do but reserve to myself a certain freedom of apprehension, arising out of the relativity of outward forms.

When we speak of 'divine guidance', we speak of what is really a very mysterious thing. It is not so much a ruling as an *over*-ruling of a process carried out through the agency of men. To be assured of its reality we have to look at the process upon a sufficiently large scale. If we take the history of the human race as a whole, we can certainly see in it a wonderful advance, and we are justified in believing that that advance has been carried out in pursuance of a great divine plan. We can go so far as to map out the outlines of this plan in broad steps or stages. But we should be wrong if we were to suppose that the forward movement was always regular and continuous. If we took our sections upon a smaller scale we should often be left in doubt whether there was any forward movement at all. Human progress, especially intellectual and spiritual progress, has always been subject to great fluctuations; it has had its ups and downs, its setbacks and retrogressions. At times the advance has been rapid; at other times it has been slow and halting; and again there have been times when there would seem to have been more of retreat than advance; ground has been lost, and has had to be recovered again.

It is one thing to believe that there is a divine guidance

in the course of events and another thing to believe that we can single out any particular series of events and claim that it represents the pure will of God without any admixture of human frailty. If we could do this, the world would not be the place of probation that it is.

If some light is thrown upon the smaller movements of mankind by comparing them with the larger, so also, conversely, light is thrown upon the larger by a study of the smaller, and even by a study of the religious history of the individual in which the search-rays are directed inwards and not outwards. The individual may be aware that there have been divine influences at work in him; but the manner in which they work, and the way in which they are blended with the subtler movements of his own nature is beyond the power of any self-analysis to disentangle.

The upshot of it all is that, if I describe the process spread out before me as one in which there are subtle veins of divine guidance, elements of permanent and eternal truth crossed and intermixed with elements of transitoriness and change, I can feel that I am describing or attempting to describe something that I can really see; I can feel that there is a rough kind of correspondence between the picture and the reality. But, if I brought in such terms as ' unalterable ' and ' infallible ', I should soon feel that my conscience ceased to bear witness with me. I should soon find myself asking ' why unalterable ? ' and ' how infallible ? '

V

I know that you have a short and easy method which disposes at one stroke of all these perplexities. You arrive *per saltum* at the perfect and final inerrancy of the whole body of Church doctrine. And you claim to have reached this by an original act of ' intuition '. You elevate your principle into an axiom which is prior to any subsequent processes of reasoning. No wonder that you are happy and content and find all the subsequent processes greatly simplified. They are really implicit in the one great premiss, which you lay down as exempt from all discussion.

Is not this method a little too easy and a little too sweeping ? I agree with you that there are some pre-suppositions which may be taken as axiomatic. The belief in the existence of the external world is such a pre-supposition. I would not dispute it if you maintain that the fundamental ideas of religion—God, Freedom, and Immortality—may be taken without proof, though I cannot really regard them as independent of reason. But I cannot in the least see that broad antecedent principles such as these supply any sound analogy or justification for the claim that you make to take on trust an elaborate system, consisting of a great number of distinct propositions, the origin and history of which is known and in regard to which the process by which they acquired authority can be retraced and tested. In such a case as this the *a priori* method is surely quite unsuitable. Logically, I can only regard your fundamental principle as a *petitio principii* on a large scale.

I must admit, however, that you make a skilful retort upon me here. You counter my criticisms by maintaining that my own vaguer belief in Providential guidance and control, as seen especially in the Old Testament and in the history of the Chosen People as the vehicle of Old Testament religion, rests upon no better basis, but is itself too assumed without proof.

The argument that I had used was an appeal to the great texts of the Old Testament which stand out in such a wonderful way as marking steps or stages in the development of what we are in the habit of calling revealed religion. These great texts are the utterances of the prophets and other religious leaders of Israel, and they claim to be spoken by divine authority and were as a matter of fact accepted as having divine authority behind them. You and I both believe that they really had this authority, which we believe to have been none the less divine because it came through human media and was exercised under human conditions without any apparent apparatus of logical proof.

I was not wholly unprepared for the construction which you put upon this fact and the use that you make of it. I had asked myself long ago what is the real place of these authoritative sayings in the great divine scheme of things. Have they any logical foothold, or do they hang entirely in the air? As they were first uttered, they carried their own authority with them; they claimed to be spoken in the name of God, and they were accepted as being really spoken in His name. You are quite within your rights in pointing out that such sayings as 'The Lord is slow to anger and plenteous in mercy', 'Like as a father pitieth his children', are by no means of the nature of direct induction from observed facts. This is perfectly true; and it is true that, if we confined ourselves to direct induction from such facts as came within our observation, we should never arrive at the central truth that 'God is Love'.

But direct induction is not the only method of proof. There is another method that is equally valid and equally normal. In the case of induction, the facts are collected and a definite conclusion is drawn from them; the facts come first and the conclusion comes last. But the process may be inverted with equal validity. We may start with the conclusion, and then verify it by a number of examples. This is the formal justification for many of the beliefs that occupy the place of first principles in the Christian religion. That God is Love, is a principle of this kind. It may be called an *anticipated truth*. It is a truth that is not obvious at first sight; but once assumed, it may be verified indefinitely, until the strong assurance is reached that it would be verified completely if we were able to follow the whole course of things.

And this is the real reason why this alternative method is so much more appropriate to the subject-matter than that of direct induction. It must never be forgotten that we men, as Bishop Butler used to say, find ourselves stranded in the midst of ' a scheme imperfectly comprehended '. What we see around us and are capable of studying directly, is only part of a much vaster whole. The conclusions that we might be tempted to draw from the little that we can see are subject to correction from the context that is unseen. But God has revealed to us enough, through the various modes of His operation, to put us in the way of verifying many a truth that would not be self-evident in its immediate context, but becomes self-evident in its relation to the larger whole that has been gradually built up by the religious experience of the race, and especially of that portion of the human race which He would seem to have chosen as typical and representative of the race ; in other words, by the religious experience of Christians.

I cannot therefore admit that the series of greater truths which form as it were the underside of Christianity are really devoid of proof or dependent upon a merely unverified intuition. What we call ' intuition ' often includes a great amount of sub-conscious and unconscious reasoning ; and the intuition of which we have been speaking is often largely of that kind.

I am quite willing to share with you the benefit of these considerations. After all, we recognize that we are largely agreed. And I am prepared to believe that there may be a good deal of semi-conscious reasoning included in the ' intuition ' on which you base your own position. But you seem to me, if I may say so, to make the mistake of claiming too much—more than can be legitimately given. And the chief reason why I prefer my position to yours, is because it does not do this. The verification is more complete ; it seems to fit the whole body of the phenomena much better.

VI

I must not forget, however, that you meet me on this ground. You urge—perhaps naturally—that the question between us is a question as to facts, and that facts are by the nature of the case unalterable. You take as an instance the assassination of Marat by Charlotte Corday. No lapse of time can alter this. It is either true or false; and if it is true, it is true for ever. And then, you argue further, that the Virgin Birth and the Resurrection are as much facts as the Crucifixion. We raise no question about the Crucifixion; and why should we raise any about other clauses of the Creed that are associated with it?

Such reasoning has a plausible appearance at first sight, but it will not bear examination. It is of course true that we are concerned with facts, but our immediate concern is with history, or the record of facts. The ultimate facts do not change, but our subjective attitude towards them may and does largely change. I have already spoken of this, in speaking of history as a subject of study. I instanced the case of the youth of Cyrus; I pointed out that the story of his youth is no longer written on the basis of the *Cyropaedia*. That is a much nearer analogy than the case of Charlotte Corday.

From the point of view of history—which is also the point of view of belief—there is a great difference between facts. Some are perfectly simple and of the kind that, as you rightly say, has to be 'taken or left'. They are directly amenable to testimony, and the testimony offered is ample and satisfactory. The Crucifixion is a fact of this order, but not so the Virgin Birth or the Resurrection. In both these cases, the portion of the statement amenable to direct testimony is relatively small; the rest is made up of inference and conjecture. The so-called fact is no longer a simple or hard fact, but includes a large amount of speculation; and to this speculative element the attitude of the twentieth century is quite different from that of the first. In the meantime there has sprung up a stricter criticism of documents and the whole new science of Comparative Religion. It is here that the difference comes in, and that the old traditional verdicts have to be reviewed and tested. There is nothing wanton or arbitrary in the process; it has become quite inevitable.

You will perhaps say that neither criticism nor comparative study present a clear enough verdict to upset the old tradition. That is the real point at issue. I do not say that they upset the whole of it, but only that part which is most speculative.

If you tell me that even this speculative portion is too important to have been left by God subject to doubt and uncertainty, I should reply by an appeal to Bishop Butler. I should submit that we never can know beforehand what God will do and what He will not do. *A priori* judgements of this kind are constantly being proved wrong.

Our object is, not to lay down what we think ought to be or what ought not, but to describe as truthfully and exactly as possible what actually is. That is really the sum and substance of any attempt at reconstruction that I have tried to make myself. I have done it in the first instance for my own satisfaction under the gradual pressure of the experience and thought of a lifetime. And I have ventured to put so much of it as I have into print in the hope that it might be helpful to others whose experience and point of view at all resemble my own.

I speak only for myself; or—so far as I can in any degree pretend to speak in the name of others besides myself—we speak only for ourselves. It is really an attempt to meet a new demand, corresponding to a comparatively advanced state of civilization. In old times people have been content to say in general terms—very often in terms inherited from the past—what they believed. But in these modern days, with the growing sensitiveness of the intellectual conscience, they feel under an obligation to say distinctly not only what they believe but in what precise sense they believe it. This does indeed perhaps open up a certain risk of collision with some of those who under different conditions would express their own beliefs differently. The remedy seems to lie in the corresponding growth of a large degree of mutual tolerance and respect for the opinions of others on the part of all who agree to meet in common acceptance of the broadly worded confessions of the past.

VII

In all that I have just been saying the idea of Relative Truth, or of the relative expression of Truth, is an essential part. The scheme of Divine Providence is a progressive scheme. Truth has been implanted among us in the form of germs, which have gone on growing and developing. But the expression of truth at each successive stage from the very first has been strictly related and proportioned to the sum of intellectual development attained at the time to which it belonged. It simply *is* so, and has been so, and no amount of theoretic manipulation on our part can make it otherwise.

There are indeed differences of degree according to the nature of the subject-matter. Some religious truths are capable of being expressed in a more permanent form than others. When Israel had reached the stage at which it was possible to formulate the moral duty of man in that concise sentence, ' Thou shalt love the Lord thy God with all thy heart and with all thy soul and with all thy strength, and thy neighbour as thyself ', that was the very climax of brevity and simplicity along with richness of potential import. But there were other truths that had to be conveyed more gradually and embodied in more complex and subtler definitions.

Take as an example that central doctrine from which we derive our very name of Christians. This name really is for us an important and fundamental element in the fabric of our beliefs. We are the 'people of the Messiah, the Lord's Anointed'. There are those who tell us that this idea of the Messiah and of divine anointing has done its work and is obsolete, that it is a rag of Judaism adhering to Christianity. It is wrong and unfilial to speak thus, though the centre of gravity has somewhat shifted and we fall back more naturally on other terms to express the same thing. The test point is that the conception of the Messiah certainly formed an integral and important part of the consciousness of our Lord Himself; it had a living meaning for Him. He had a real need of it to express to Himself the secret of His own Being, and to convey that secret to the intelligence of a part at least of the world around Him. The Christian of to-day, when he seeks the highest sanction for his own beliefs, goes reverently over the whole ground. He looks reverently into the mirror of that Divine consciousness, and he tries to apply to himself and assimilate what he sees there. He is constantly paraphrasing for his own use in various connexions the famous lines:

> What that Word doth make it
> That I believe and take it.

The emphasis may fall differently, but the intention is throughout the same.

Another of the old fundamental conceptions comes back to us; and here again we have substantially the same conditions. What the doctrine of the Messiah was for our Lord Himself, that the philosophical doctrine of the Logos was for the next and succeeding generations of His disciples. For them this doctrine was full of varied suggestiveness and help, though it would be too much to claim that it was an absolutely perfect and final expression of the truth that it was intended to convey. Different ages have in like manner made use of different formulations and ideas, all subsidiary to the same result, though none of them exactly coincided with and exhausted that result. Down to this present time it may be doubted whether either the Church of Christ as a whole or any individual Christian, even the most learned and the most philosophical, has really arrived at an absolutely perfect expression for that which all alike, both the Body and the members, have been struggling both to express for themselves and to formulate for the use of others. They are still in the position that they can afford to neglect or despise none of the achievements of the past. Those achievements may have been partial, and elements in them may have been provisional and transitory, but they were all ingredients —and valuable ingredients—in the manifold and multiform whole. We do not know what the future may have in store for us. There may set in a period of greater concentration and simplification of which some coming generation or generations may reap the benefit. Our duty is, in the meanwhile, to make the best use we can of that which we have ourselves inherited from the past and as good stewards to hand it on to our successors.

It will be seen from such a sketch as this why I and those whoever they may be, whether many or few, who agree with me, so strongly deprecate the whole idea of denials. The Christian effort after the formulation of divine truth must be taken as a whole in all its successive historical phases. We need it as a whole, apprehended in all its various degrees, if it is to take shape for us in any sort of completeness.

In such a condition of things, denial is only too apt to mean mutilation; and the attitude of denial is just the wrong, and not the right, attitude. *Der Geist der stets verneint* is the spirit of Mephistopheles and not of the Christian. Our enemies and a few of our too-zealous friends, through a mistake of judgement, try to inveigle us into denials, but we steadily refuse to be either drawn or driven into them.

To abstain from certain affirmations is an altogether different thing. That may be only the response of a sensitive conscience to the recognition of altered conditions. It may be only an incident in the inevitable process of adjustment. The particular detail that seems to drop out may be abundantly compensated for by the enlarged significance of some other detail which remains behind. As I said just now, it may be nothing more than a change of emphasis; in other words, no change of substance, but only a certain shifting in the play of light and shade.

This, and not any other, is the kind of position which I and those who think with me desire to defend. We wish to be judged upon our merits, and not with reference to any one else. For that reason I would submit to you that Troeltsch and his allies may be left out of the question. Their aims are not ours, and the limits within which we desire to work are not theirs.

The real ground on which we are prepared to be judged is the ground of consistency with objective and verifiable facts. We aim at taking the fullest possible account of these, no matter from what side they come. Our range is catholic. There is no form or kind of reality that we consider alien to us, whether spiritual or material. We only feel bound to apply rather strict tests as to what is reality and what is not. Subject to these tests, we aim at sacrificing neither the old to the new nor the new to the old. Our theology is still, in all essentials, the theology of St. Paul and St. John; what they laid stress upon, we also lay stress upon; our view of the spiritual world aspires to be, both in whole and parts, fundamentally the same as theirs. We believe that this view is firmly anchored in the innermost heart of things. But at the same time we claim the right to express to ourselves the Apostolic teaching in the language that is most natural to the century in which we live. Without this right we should feel that our own assent to it was forced and strained and not more than half sincere. For us there is no dilemma ; because we maintain that the two sides of our faith not only can be but have been reconciled. All that we need to do is to set them frankly side by side. We render to Caesar the things that are Caesar's, and to God the things that are God's, as we hope in just and due proportions, not forgetting that the latter includes the former and that what we call Caesar and all his works is but a form of the one great Divine self-manifestation.

Yours very sincerely,

W. SANDAY.

MR. N. P. WILLIAMS' CONCLUDING LETTER

My dear Dr. Sanday,
       The task which lies before me now is a somewhat difficult one. I have to reply to the criticisms directed by you in your last letter against my position, or such parts of my position as you do not feel able to accept : and you will no doubt expect me to reply to the best of my ability ; but, on the other hand, my answer must be phrased in such a way as not to place you under the necessity of sending me yet another rejoinder, for so our correspondence might be prolonged *ad infinitum*. Perhaps, however, I may console myself with the reflection that (if this correspondence is to be published) you will in reality have the last word, as it will fall to you to write an Introduction ; and this consideration will doubtless justify my writing with rather more liberty than I might have otherwise felt able to assume.

I

Before addressing myself to the consideration of the cardinal points at issue between us, I should like to comment briefly on your remarks with regard to ' authority ' and ' truth ', contained in section I of your last letter (p. 94). You say ' For me, the ultimate standard of judgement is what I conceive to be Truth. Authority has its weight ; but I could not accept a thing purely upon authority, if I did not also believe it to be true. With me, the idea of Truth stands behind everything else ; with you, if I am not mistaken, the idea of Authority sometimes takes precedence and becomes a ground of acceptance independently of truth.' I hope you will not think that

I am being unduly captious : but, to my mind, these words sound as though you thought that *I* am not also interested primarily in Truth. Obviously, one can only ' accept ' a proposition because one believes it to be ' true ' : it would require quite inconceivable mental perversity to ' accept ' a statement which one knew to be false, merely because it was promulgated by authority. Of course, as I have explained before, the fact that certain statements are vouched for by ' Authority ' is, on our view, good evidence for their truth ; but it is, in theory, conceivable that this kind of evidence might be cancelled by absolutely indubitable and irrefutable evidence provided by the senses, or by some rigorous and exact chain of reasoning ; in which case, the statements in question would fall to the ground, and the whole fabric of ' Authority ' with them. As I have said before, I believe in the Virgin Birth (*a*) because the Church and the Scriptures say that it was so, (*b*) because it seems to me appropriate and congruous to the idea of a Divine Incarnation that it should have been so, and (*c*) because I know of no good reason for disbelieving that it was so ; but *if* a papyrus were discovered at Nazareth which proved, beyond the shadow of a doubt, that our Lord was not born of a virgin, I should at once and without hesitation abandon, not merely the belief in the Virgin Birth, but all the rest of Catholic Christianity as well. Such a declaration as this ought, in my opinion, to vindicate me and those who think with me from any charge, or even suggestion, of indifference to truth. When you say, ' The Modernist . . . aims above all things at the highest kind of (truth and sincerity) : he does not think that he has attained to the highest truth or the highest sincerity until he can speak from personal conviction,' you are affirming what I have never doubted : it is, perhaps, not impertinent to add that the love of truth and sincerity is not the Modernist's monopoly. The most convinced Traditionalist can heartily subscribe to the maxim, *Deus mendacio nostro non indiget*. Of course the point is a purely verbal one, for I do not suppose for a moment that you really mean to accuse us of putting the interests of authority first, and the interests of truth second : but, as you say, 'for complete mutual understanding, it is as well to be quite explicit.'

II

The first point of importance which claims attention is the question of 'modern methods of writing history', and the influence which they are entitled to exert upon the form (as distinct from the content) of Christian beliefs at the present day. I understand you to contend as follows :—

(1) Within the last hundred years a ' complete revolution ' has taken place in the art of writing history. The methods of textual, literary, and historical criticism have been improved, sharpened, and raised to a degree of efficiency and certitude hitherto undreamed of.

(2) In many domains of history, the application of these improved critical methods to the documentary sources has resulted in a complete *bouleversement* of the traditional view. This has been conspicuously the case in regard to the Old Testament. Many narratives contained in the Old Testament Canon are now regarded as belonging to the sphere of legend rather than to that of history ; and, even in the case of those narratives which are recognized as strictly historical, the whole perspective has been altered, so that what the narratives represent as primitive is now seen to be the product of later development, projected by the imagination of the devout into the past.

(3) It is therefore to be expected *a priori* that the application of modern critical methods to the books of the New Testament will have the same results as in the case of the Old—that some narratives will be discovered to be rather of the nature of poetical legend than of exact

history, and that in the case of the others the balance and perspective of the historical scheme will be considerably modified.

I am afraid that I must entirely dispute the cogency of this argument. Because *some* ancient documents which profess to be history have been discovered to be romance, it does not follow that *all* will be. To quote your own instance—it would clearly be fallacious to argue that because Xenophon's *Cyropaedia* is largely romance, *therefore* Tacitus's life of Agricola must be expected *a priori* to be largely romance. Because Herodotus is admittedly full of legendary stories, it does not follow that Thucydides must be expected to be full of legendary stories. I do not suppose, of course, that you regard this part of your argument as constituting a rigorously exact syllogism, because it would obviously involve an 'undistributed middle', viz. the term 'ancient documents'. But even if you mean (as I do not doubt that you do mean) only to claim for your conclusion a general antecedent probability, and not mathematical certainty, I fear that I cannot concede even this. I cannot admit any cogency whatever in the contention ' because some portions of the Old Testament are admittedly poetry rather than history, it is therefore antecedently probable that some portions of the New Testament are poetry rather than history'. It may be so: but we shall only admit that it is so when compelled by the best of objective and *a posteriori* evidence. And this it seems to me that you fail to supply. In your last letter you content yourself with stating, ' I confess that I do not think it too soon to let our general view of the New Testament be affected by our general view of the Old ' . . . (p. 98). ' I have no doubt in my own mind that the process begun in reference to the Old Testament must be carried forward to the New ' (ibid.) ; but the matter is clearly not one that can be settled by an *ipse dixit*. We (that is, those who think with me) are constrained to demand that each document of the New Testament Canon shall be judged on its merits and without prejudice ; and, as I said in my last letter, if the result of a scientific and dispassionate investigation is to disprove the historicity of the events which they narrate, we are prepared to take the consequences, and to jettison the beliefs which rest upon these (alleged) events ; but we cannot acquiesce in what we should naturally regard, from the point of view of exact logic, as a quiet begging of the whole question before it has been adequately discussed.

I must needs feel that a certain ambiguity lurks in the sentence which I have just quoted, ' I have no doubt in my own mind that the process begun in reference to the Old Testament must be carried forward to the New ' (p. 98). There is a sense in which I could heartily accept this proposition and make it my own, and another sense in which I should be compelled emphatically to disagree with it. It all depends upon what you mean by ' the process begun in reference to the Old Testament '. If you merely mean that the same critical *methods* must be employed for fixing the text of the New Testament, for determining the sources of its narratives, and for evaluating the historical character of these sources, as have been employed in the case of the Old Testament, I heartily agree : that is, with the proviso that these critical methods shall be used with the sanity and sobriety which distinguishes the work of the best British scholars, such, for instance, as the late Dr. Driver. I have no desire to warn off criticism, as such, from the field of the New Testament. But if you mean that ' the process begun in reference to the Old Testament ' must be ' carried forward to the New ', in the sense that criticism must consciously aim at producing a *bouleversement* of New Testament tradition similar to that which has been undergone by Old Testament tradition, I must beg leave to disagree. I have no objection to the same processes being applied to the New Testament as have been applied to the Old Testament : what I object to is the *a priori* assumption that the results of these processes ought to be, or necessarily will be, similar in both cases.

III

This point, again, that I have just been discussing is, I suppose, only a verbal one. I do not imagine that you wish to prescribe ' Liberal ' conclusions beforehand, to be arrived at by the critic, any more than I should wish to prescribe ' orthodox ' conclusions to the critic, *as such*. Perhaps I might say a few words about the relation which, in my view, the personal convictions of the critic ought to bear to the exercise of his functions *as* critic, for the purpose of clearing up any obscurities which may arise. I approach the New Testament documents, being myself already possessed of and believing in the Catholic Faith. If I am going to use the sacred text for devotional or homiletic purposes, I keep my Faith well in the forefront of my mind, and endeavour to relate every thought and aspiration of the inspired writers to the eternal verities which the Church has taught me. On the other hand, if I am purposing to handle the documents, not as a Christian priest or preacher, but merely as a critical student, I endeavour as far as I can to keep my Faith at the back of my mind—to abstract my intellectual activities from the influence of the Faith which I do as a matter of fact hold—to judge questions of textual authenticity and historical fact simply on the evidence, with as near an approximation to unbiased impartiality as I can attain to. Having arrived at my historical conclusions, I should then compare them with the historical statements to which the Faith commits me ; if the former were to appear prima facie contradictory to the latter, I should retrace my steps, and go over my chain of reasoning again, testing each link, and endeavouring to find a weak place ; and if I were to find that the contradiction could not by any means be removed—that the historical statements of the

Faith proved to be in opposition to absolutely certain facts—then I should without hesitation renounce a Faith which I had found to be untrue.

IV

I had not wished to be drawn into a discussion on the subject of Miracles, as I have already expressed my opinions on this question elsewhere. Moreover, I did not wish to trespass on the ground of your debate with the Dean of Christ Church. But the argument seems to have drifted, by a sort of inevitable necessity, in that direction, so that I am constrained to say a few words on the subject before our correspondence closes.

Let me briefly resume the situation, as I understand it. In my second letter (p. 85), I designated, as one of the two root-differences which divide us, a divergence of opinion as to the intrinsic possibility or probability of certain miracles. I had gathered from your original paper that, whilst not wishing to deny the possibility of ' miracle ' in general, you had felt that an ' imperious necessity ' compelled you to ' abstain from affirming ' two particular miracles, namely, the alleged birth of Jesus Christ from a maiden, and His alleged corporeal Resurrection from the tomb. This ' imperious necessity ', you contend, is rooted in the fact that these two wonders would be definitely *contra*, and not merely *supra, naturam*. I ventured to hint (in my second letter) that I had really not an idea as to what you meant by the words ' *contra* ', ' *supra* ', and ' *natura* '. Perhaps I may now be permitted to examine the reply contained in your last communication.

V

You say, in the first place, that your object in drawing the distinction between *supra naturam* and *contra naturam* miracles was ' not scientific, but practical '—and that you thought that the distinction ' would convey a sufficiently clear meaning to ordinary people'. I do not know whether those who think with me can claim to be 'ordinary people': but I am afraid I must say that we are not to be converted by language of a merely 'practical' nature. If we are to drop, or consider the possibility of dropping, beliefs on which our whole lives have hitherto been built, we must be constrained thereto by the most indubitable and undeniable facts, or by reasoning of an absolutely stringent and rigorous character, based upon indubitable facts. We can only be evicted from our trenches at the point of the bayonet.

This, however, is merely by the way, and I must proceed to consider the definition of '*natura*' which you supply in your last letter. You say 'By "nature" I meant what are commonly called "the laws of matter and motion"' (p. 99): and I presume that when, later on, you speak of 'the ordinary course of nature' and 'the natural order' (p. 100), the word 'nature' is meant to be understood in the same sense.

When I read this definition ('nature = the laws of matter and motion') I seemed instantaneously to see a whole train of implications flowing from it, which, I imagine, you would be very loth to accept. In order, however, to avoid any suspicion of an unfair use of your words, I took the liberty of submitting this part of your argument to a distinguished philosophical teacher in this University, and asked him, 'What would *you* understand by "the laws of matter and motion?"' He replied, 'I should naturally take this to mean "the laws of physics and chemistry"'; and this was, as a matter of fact, the meaning which I had at first sight attached to the phrase. If, then, your language is to be taken at its face value, it would seem that the laws of physics and chemistry constitute the criterion whereby the credibility of particular miracles is to be judged. But, if this position is to be taken as axiomatic, it must be pointed out that its consequences are somewhat far-reaching. If capacity for being explained by the laws of physics and chemistry is the criterion for judging of the reality of ' miracles ', *a fortiori* it must be the criterion for judging of the reality of all alleged events whatsoever. Because a ' miracle ' (on your showing) is merely a ' wonder ' (p. 99) which lies ' outside the common order ' (ibid.)—that is, presumably, outside the usual experience of mankind. But this simply means that a ' miracle ' is a surprising event. Now the term ' surprising ' is clearly a relative term : events may be surprising to one man which are not surprising to another. The passage of an aeroplane across the sky, which awakens no amazement in the breast of a modern European, would occasion the extremest surprise and astonishment to an Andaman islander. Clearly, then, the ' surprisingness ' of a miracle is not something inherent in the miracle ; it is a ' separable accident ', which has nothing to do with the τί ἦν εἶναι of the miracle itself.

Consequently, if ' explicability by the laws of physics and chemistry ' is the test of reality in the case of alleged ' miracles ' or ' surprising ' events, it can only be because it is the test of reality in the case of all alleged events whatsoever.

VI

But when we have reached this point in the process of tracing out the implications of your identification of ' nature ' with ' the laws of matter and motion ', it would seem that we can no longer avoid conclusions which are utterly fatal to, and destructive of, religion in general, and the Christian religion in particular. For if the real is that, and that only, which is explicable by the laws of physics and chemistry, what becomes of personality, thought, religious experience, consciousness, and life itself ? They are mere *epiphenomena*, mere aspects of physical and chemical processes which presumably have no substantive existence apart from those processes. We seem landed in an iron materialism, in which all modes of spiritual existence appear to be nothing but ways of describing the blind, purposeless clash of colliding atoms. The conceptions of free self-determining personality and of a life beyond the grave would seem to be decisively excluded: how can the 'soul', if it is merely a name for certain aspects of a physico-chemical process, persist in isolation when that process has come to end? How can an 'aspect' survive the dissolution of the substantive reality whereof it is an aspect?

I am quite sure that you would repudiate such a mechanistic *Weltanschauung* as heartily as I should myself: indeed, you have done so in your original paper (p. 18). But it seems to be irresistibly implied in the setting up of the laws of physics and chemistry as the ultimate criterion of reality in respect of 'surprising events'. I must therefore have been wrong in my prima facie assumption that by your phrase 'the laws of matter and motion' you meant 'the laws of physics and chemistry'. But, if this is so, I have not the least idea what you mean by 'the laws of matter and motion', and am, therefore, just as much in the dark as ever about the sense in which you are using the word '*natura*'. The fault is doubtless mine: but I am afraid I must say that, in defining ' natura ' as ' the laws of matter and motion' you have (so far as I am concerned) merely defined *ignotum per ignotius*.

VII

It is possible, however, that you might reply to this argument as follows:—

'Not so fast. It is perfectly true that by " the laws of matter and motion " I meant the laws of physics and chemistry, or the laws of physics only. But you are not justified in assuming that I regard " complete explicability by the laws of physics and chemistry " as the criterion of reality in the case of " surprising events ". I did not say that "surprising events", in order to be accepted as having really happened, must prove that they are susceptible of a *complete* explanation by these laws: I merely said that they must not involve a *breach* of these laws. It is quite possible for a phenomenon to be only partially explicable in physical or chemical terms, without, nevertheless, *contradicting* the well-ascertained laws of the universe which are embodied in the sciences of physics and chemistry.' But is it? Let us briefly examine the meaning of these terms ' breach' and ' contradiction'.

VIII

I hope I shall not be suspected of purely verbal quibbling if I say that I am not at all certain what is meant by a ' breach' or a ' contradiction' of ' the laws of matter and motion', for the purposes of rigorous reasoning. I have suggested one possible meaning for the phrase ' an event involving a " breach " of the laws of matter and motion '—namely, ' an event which is not completely explicable in terms of physics and chemistry': but, as I have just said, this is evidently not your meaning. I know well enough what is meant by a ' breach' of the laws of England: it means, roughly, disobedience to a command of the Legislature. But I need not remind you that ' the laws of nature' are not ' laws' in the juridical sense: they are statements of what is, not of what ought to be: they are existential propositions, not commands or ' value-judgements'. Now a ' contradiction' of an existential proposition would presumably mean what is known in formal logic as its ' contrary', or its ' contradictory'. For instance, the 'law of gravitation' states that ' All material bodies attract each other with a force varying inversely as the square of the distance'. The contrary of this would be '*No* material bodies attract each other, &c. . . .', and the contradictory would be '*Some* material bodies do *not* attract each other, &c. . . .'. An event, therefore, which ' involved a breach of' the law of gravitation, would be an event, belief in which would commit us to the acceptance either of the proposition ' *No* material bodies attract each other, &c.' or of the proposition ' Some material bodies do not attract each other'. Now I should contend that no such event is recorded, either in Holy Scripture, or in the lives of the saints, or even in the wildest records of hagiographical imagination. I know of no alleged 'miracle' which necessarily involves a 'contradiction', in this sense, of the law of gravitation.

This may, perhaps, be regarded as a somewhat startling assertion, in view of the innumerable stories of 'levitation' which occur in the Old Testament, the New Testament, and subsequent ecclesiastical history. But I must repeat that no alleged instance of 'levitation', in itself, and necessarily, involves a 'breach' or 'contradiction' of the law of gravitation. Perhaps a parable will help me to explain what I mean.

IX

Suppose that I were to relate the following anecdote to a Modernist theologian. ' The other day, I was present at a cricket match, and witnessed a curious phenomenon. Jones was batting. A slow ball came along : Jones stepped out from his crease, and smote with all his might. From the surface of his bat the ball soared away in a graceful parabola : it reached the summit of its trajectory, and dipped downward towards the earth. However, when it arrived at a point about five feet from the ground, it stopped dead, and remained suspended motionless in the air.' If my supposed theologian was an exceptionally unsuspicious person, he might perhaps retort ' Nonsense. Your story is on the face of it untrue. " Imperious necessity " compels me to reject it ; for the supposition of a ball stopping dead in the air whilst falling towards the earth would involve a breach or contradiction of the law of gravitation—it would be *contra naturam*.' To which

I might reply ' Well, this event, of which you deny the possibility, certainly happened. As a matter of fact the ball was caught by one of the fielding side. The law of gravitation was not " broken " or repealed when " mid-off " caught the ball in its flight towards the earth : the earth did not suddenly cease to exert the force of its attraction upon the ball : what happened was that this force was counteracted and neutralized by an opposing force, exerted by the muscles of " mid-off's " hand upon the surface of the ball : and this latter opposing force, though it may be partially explicable in physical or chemical terms, was set in motion by a purely spiritual cause, namely, the will of Robinson to " catch " Jones " out ".' There is, therefore, nothing inherently impossible about the conception of a natural force being temporarily neutralized or counteracted by other forces set in motion by spiritual causes : it is a thing which happens every day, which we ourselves are perpetually bringing to pass in all our dealing with and handling of the material world.

' Quite so,' perhaps you will say ; ' I quite admit that the operation of natural forces can be suspended or interfered with by spiritual causes, whether human or superhuman, and instances of such suspension or interference are exactly what I mean by *supra naturam* events. What I deny is the possibility that natural forces could be, not merely transcended or superseded, but actually abolished or annihilated, even though such abolition or annihilation were alleged to have been merely temporary. Alleged events of this nature are what I should describe as *contra naturam* '. Let me for a moment consider this position.

Our Divine Saviour is said in the Gospels on one occasion to have walked or moved, in His physical body, across and above the surface of the Lake of Gennesaret : and the same is recorded of several Christian saints in later centuries, such as St. Hyacinth of Poland and St. Raymund of Pennafort. I imagine that I should not be acting unfairly if I were to assume that you would stamp these alleged events without more ado as *contra naturam*. But are they ? I am not, for the moment, discussing the question whether they really happened : I am simply concerned to inquire whether, *if* they happened, they would have involved the (temporary) annihilation, or merely the neutralization, of natural forces. And it is clear (at any rate to my mind) that these alleged events do not necessarily involve more than the counteraction of natural forces by spiritual forces, or by other natural forces set in motion by spiritual causes. Suppose, for the moment, that our Lord did walk upon the waters : it would not be necessary to assume that the force of the earth's attraction ceased to exist so far as His Body was concerned : it would be quite as easy to say that this force was counteracted and neutralized by spiritual energies belonging to the unseen world, or by natural forces set in motion by such energies. The case would be exactly analogous to that of the cricket ball, except that the spiritual cause which neutralized the force of the earth's attraction would be superhuman, and not merely human. In other words, the alleged miracle of the walking upon the water can quite reasonably be represented as *supra naturam*.

But, if this is so, a consequence of considerable logical importance follows, which I will endeavour to explain.

In the foregoing discussion, I have taken the example of the law of gravitation and the alleged miracles of levitation, because these miracles were adduced by you in your original paper as instances of *contra naturam* events which could and should be dogmatically condemned *a priori* (p. 16 : ' We are convinced that life in New Testament times was not conducted as if in the atmosphere of a dark séance. We are convinced that bodies in those days did not float in the air or materialize and dematerialize at will '). But the same line of reasoning seems to hold good with regard to all the alleged events which I understand that you would stamp as *contra naturam*. Multiplications of food, bilocations, resuscitations of the dead—all *could* be represented as involving, not the ' contradiction ' of natural laws, but their temporary supersession by supernatural laws. So far as I know, there is no alleged wonder recorded in Holy Scripture and the lives of the saints which might not be explained, with a little ingenuity, as involving—not the annihilation of natural forces, but —their counteraction and neutralization by spiritual forces, or by other natural forces set in motion by spiritual causes. (Let me say again, in order to avoid misunderstanding, that I am very far from asserting that all these alleged wonders *did* actually happen : I am merely contending in the abstract that the *hypothesis* of their having happened would not necessarily and inherently involve the hypothesis of a ' contradiction ' of ' the laws of nature '.) Even the most fantastic products of hagiographical fancy need not necessarily be described as inherently *contra naturam*, for it could always be contended by the hagiographer that the particular wonder proposed by him for our acceptance was merely an instance of the neutralization and not of the annihilation of natural forces. I have no doubt that even ' Joshua's moon in Ajalon ', or the flying house of Loretto, could be represented in this way, were it worth anybody's while to do so.

If, then, the term ' *contra* ' is understood in the sense which I have affixed to it, it would seem that there are literally no alleged miracles, not even the most outrageous, which can be pronounced at once and without more ado as '*contra naturam*' (*natura* being understood as = the laws of physics and chemistry). All alleged miracles, it would seem, are only *supra naturam*, and the *contra naturam* test seems to fall to the ground. On the other hand, if my interpretation of the word *contra* is incorrect, I am utterly at a loss to know what is the true interpretation.

X

Perhaps I may summarize the above criticism of your position as follows :—

1. You object to alleged ' miracles ' which are ' *contra*, and not merely *supra* ', *naturam*.

    I inquire what you mean by these terms.

2. You reply that by *natura* you mean ' the laws of matter and motion ' (but you omit to explain what you mean by *supra* and *contra*—which is the real point).

3. I naturally take ' the laws of matter and motion ' to mean ' the ·laws of physics and chemistry '—at least, if the phrase does not mean this, I do not know what it means.

4. Assuming, however, that this identification is correct (' the laws of matter and motion = ' the laws of physics and chemistry ') I am still not certain what is meant by the preposition *contra* or the verb ' to contradict ', in reference to ' *natura* ' or ' the laws of matter and motion '.

5. The first idea that occurs to me is that by ' an alleged event which *contradicts* the laws of matter and motion (i. e. of physics and chemistry) ' you mean an event which is not completely and exhaustively explicable in terms of those Laws. A little consideration, however, shows me that this cannot be so, inasmuch as it would presuppose a thoroughgoing Materialism which I am very sure that you do not hold.

6. I must therefore conclude that by an alleged event which ' contradicts ' the law specified above you mean an event which could only have happened if the natural forces, of which these laws are compendious and more or less imperfect descriptions, had been (temporarily) *abolished* or *annihilated*. But I am then faced with the difficulty that no

alleged miracles, not even those which I should hold to be most inconsistent with the revealed character of God, seem to be in this sense *contra naturam* : there is no alleged wonder, however grotesque, which could not be represented as involving, not the annihilation, but the neutralization of natural forces.

7. It would seem to follow that the distinction between *supra naturam* and *contra naturam* is solely a difference of terminology : every alleged superhuman interference, and indeed every actual human interference, with the operation of mechanical laws, could equally well be described from one point of view as *supra* and from another point of view as *contra naturam*. Consequently, if we are willing to follow the argument whithersoever it leads, the attempt to label some alleged miracles as *supra naturam* and others as *contra naturam* would appear to be purely arbitrary.

XI

A few words may now be devoted to another possible definition of '*contra naturam* events', which might be inferred from your language on p. 100. Speaking of ' well-attested ' and ' *supra naturam* events ' you say that such events have all had ' analogies in the ordinary course of nature ' ; it might, therefore, be concluded that you would define ' *contra naturam* events ' as events which have no analogies in the ordinary course of nature. But what is an ' analogy ' ? As used in ordinary speech, the term ' analogy ' is one of the vaguest words in the English language. I doubt whether it can be taken to mean more than a vague sort of resemblance or similarity. And again, it would, I think, be difficult to quote an instance of an alleged miracle for which an ' analogy ', in the sense of an event bearing some sort of hazy resemblance or parallelism to it, could not be discovered in the ordinary course of nature. If this kind of argument has any real value, it would not be difficult to produce ' analogies ' from nature to *parthenogenesis* and the production of new life out of death. No doubt you remember the late Prof. Drummond's *Natural Law in the Spiritual World*, which was devoted to the development of just such an analogical argument in favour of the Gospel miracles. I never could discern very much weight in this contention, though it was designed to support the conclusions which I should wish to advocate; nor do I find any more weight in it if it is turned against those conclusions. Why should not the Almighty, in the course of His extraordinary dealings with mankind, perform actions to which no exact parallel can be found in His ordinary operations in nature ? I entirely agree with your observation on p. 101, ' The evidence for this kind of regularity ' [i. e. what is commonly called the ' uniformity of nature '] ' is so overwhelming that I cannot help regarding the will that finds expression in it as deeply rooted in the character of God Himself ' : but I see no reason why this element in the character of God should be held to exclude the possibility of His possessing those qualities which in human beings we should call originality, the faculty of initiative, the power of making fresh departures. Stability of character and the power of initiative are not incompatible in men ; why should they be thought so in the case of God ?

XII

Perhaps you may think that I have devoted a disproportionate amount of space to this particular question, especially as (to judge from your language on p. 101) you would not wish to rest the main weight of your argument against the Gospel miracles upon *a priori* considerations. But it seems to me that the ground would be cleared for any future discussion if it could be agreed that the distinction between *contra naturam* and *supra naturam* miracles is, as you say, ' popular, and not scientific ' : and that consequently it would not be illegitimate to found upon this distinction any argument adverse to the particular miracles which happened to have been labelled as *contra naturam*.

XIII

For these reasons I am unable to find very much cogency in the *a priori* part of your argument against the Gospel miracles, understood in the traditional way. I quite admit that as a matter of psychological fact the observed regularity of nature does create in the normal human mind a real *praeiudicium* (though, as I should contend, a *praeiudicium* which should be frankly recognized as provisional) against the historicity of any supposed events which would involve the supersession of natural forces by causes belonging to an alleged spiritual world ; but, if we are willing to remember that

There are more things in heaven and earth, Horatio,
Than are dreamt of in your philosophy,

such a *praeiudicium* cannot be described as overwhelming, or sufficient to condemn a particular miracle even before the *a posteriori* evidence for it has been heard. I do not think that any one would be justified (unless, indeed, he started from avowedly materialistic and atheistic presuppositions) in doing more than ' pencilling a note of interrogation in the margin ' of the record of an alleged event of this nature, and passing on. The only *a priori* test which, in my opinion, can be reasonably employed to condemn alleged miracles without more ado—which justifies us in refusing even to consider the evidence for them—is that of consonance with what we believe (on other grounds) to be the character of God. You have said, in another connexion, that ' we never can know beforehand what God will do and what He will not do ' (p. 113) : but is not this, perhaps, a little too sweeping ? We should both agree, I imagine, that He is not likely to work absurd, trivial, or immoral miracles. It is this consideration which justifies us in ruling out of court at once such stories as that of the Virgin taking the place of the runaway nun, or the parrot, who, when pursued by a hawk, screamed out '*Sancte Thoma ora pro nobis*', with the result that his pursuer fell dead. For believers in the Christian God this criterion approaches as nearly to absolute cogency as any *a priori* test can : though of course there may be a large field of alleged wonders, in regard to which we cannot feel certain whether or not they are too trivial for Almighty God to have worked. This last consideration would, however, not apply to the crucial miracles of the Gospel (i. e. the Virgin Birth, Resurrection, and Ascension) which, whether true or not, are clearly not trivial or unimportant.

I have said before that if I approached the consideration of the Gospel miracles, believing generally in God, but without any further presuppositions, I do not think I should be justified in condemning them off-hand as legends : what I should do would be ' to pencil a note of interrogation in the margin, and pass on '. You may say, ' But that is exactly what I am doing : I do not condemn, or deny, these miracles : I merely label them with a query and devote myself to affirming the other parts of the Christian creed which do not seem to require any such labelling '. To which I may reply, quite frankly : ' Quite so : I should do exactly the same, but for my fundamental postulate of the " infallibility of the Church " '—which I will proceed to discuss presently.

Before doing this, however, I must devote a few lines to what you claim (on p. 101) as having been, for you, ' the really determining trains of argument '—namely, ' those which have come from the side of history and criticism or from that of psychology.' Perhaps I may be permitted, for the sake of clearness and brevity, to employ once more the method of first summarizing your contentions and then commenting on them.

XIV

If I understand it rightly, your argument runs as follows :—

1. In the case of Old Testament miracles, there is no 'authentic first-hand testimony' for the reality of details which would have involved 'a real contradiction of the laws of nature'; in other words, for *contra naturam* miracles. All the records which we possess were written many years or centuries after the events : and there is a strong probability in the nature of things that legendary details would creep in. The occurrence of *'contra naturam'* miracles in Old Testament times is, therefore, not proven.

2. A similar line of reasoning may be applied to the miracles of the New Testament. 'The first-class evidence, that of St. Paul's epistles, is available only for miracles of the first order '—i. e. *supra naturam* miracles. In the case of alleged *contra naturam* details, although the interval between the occurrence of the facts and the composition of the records was not so great as in the Old Testament, there was nevertheless ample time for the growth of legendary accretions, in the process of oral, and even of literary, transmission of the narratives. The occurrence of genuinely *contra naturam* miracles in New Testament times, as in Old Testament times, is, accordingly, not proven.

3. If, however, the occurrence of *contra naturam* miracles cannot be demonstrated either in the Old or in the New Testaments, and if it is possible to explain the narratives of them as due to the unconscious operation of mythopoeic imagination, such an explanation becomes invested with a high degree of probability ; in fact ' we have no doubt in our own minds that, of the two hypotheses—

that these things really happened, and that they came to be thought to have happened on the basis of widely prevalent ideas—the latter is by far the more probable ' (p. 16).

XV

The first and most obvious comment which I have to make upon this reasoning is that it presupposes, all through, the distinction between *supra naturam* and *contra naturam* miracles which you claim to derive from the *a priori* part of your argument. This distinction is really the foundation-stone upon which the successive tiers of your argument ultimately rest. But, as I have explained just now, I am not able to accept this distinction. I cannot admit any difference, in respect of principle, between the Healing of the Blind, the Raising of the Dead, and Walking on the Sea. For me, there is only one kind, or one ' order ', of alleged miracles. By a ' miracle ' I mean an event which involves the counteraction or neutralization of natural forces by causes belonging to the spiritual world—an event which may be indifferently described as *contra* or as *supra naturam*. Consequently, the chain of reasoning by which you justify your characteristic position, i. e. that which permits you to accept some miracles and reject others, has no cogency for me.

XVI

Suppose, however, that for ' *contra naturam* miracles ' we substitute throughout your argument ' miracles in general ' : even in this form the argument would in my opinion still fall short of formal cogency.

Because the ' mythological hypothesis ' would still be only an hypothesis, in a great many cases. In some, of course, it has to be accepted, because the alternative hypothesis (viz. that the alleged miracle really happened) is, not merely unproved, but definitely disproved—as in the case of the Flood story. But nobody has ever proved, or presumably ever will be able to prove (in the sense of rigorously certain demonstration), that Elisha did *not* make the iron to swim. It may be the case that the written evidence for this incident dates from a time long after its alleged occurrence, and that the narrative looks suspiciously like folk-lore : but the fact that it *can* be explained mythologically does not prove, or demonstrate mathematically, that it *must* be so explained. I might be inclined to say, as a matter of subjective feeling and instinct, that the mythological explanation was perhaps the most probable : but, from the point of view of strictly objective and rigorous reasoning, I should not feel justified in dogmatically ruling out the other explanation, viz. that the incident really happened. In other words, my attitude would have to be one of strict agnosticism : I should have, as I said before, to ' pencil a note of interrogation in the margin, and pass on '.

And this, as a matter of fact, is the attitude which I should desire to advocate with regard to the miracles recorded in the Old Testament. A few, like the story of a universal Flood, are definitely known to be unhistorical : one or two others, like that of Jonah and the great fish, occur in narratives which we now know were not meant even by their authors to be taken as history : a few more, like the story of Elijah calling down fire from heaven upon Ahaziah's soldiery, seem definitely inconsistent with the character of God as we know it from the New Testament. But of the rest, and particularly of those miraculous narratives which cluster round the great moments in the history of the Chosen People—the Exodus, the Giving of the Law, and the Prophetic movement— I should like to say this : I do not doubt that miracles in general did occur during the period of the Old Testament and especially at these crucial points in the development of Israel's life : but I am not prepared to go to the stake for the exact historicity of any one particular miraculous

142 *Form and Content in Christian Tradition*

record precisely as it stands in the Old Testament. And that represents the exact amount of weight which I should attach to the consideration (of which I fully admit the truth) that a long space of time intervened between the occurrence of the events and the composition of the records. A firm belief in miracles in general, and a disinclination to commit myself to all the details of any one miracle in particular—this appears to me to be an attitude to take up with regard to the Old Testament which is both reasonable in itself and entirely loyal to the historical connexion and continuity between the Jewish and Christian *Ecclesiae*.

You will thus see that the view which I should desire to advocate with regard to the miracles of the Old Testament is practically very similar to, if not theoretically identical with, that which you hold with regard to certain miracles of the New Testament: and you may ask, ' Why not frankly go forward upon the same lines ' ? To which I should reply, that the cases of the Old Testament miracles and of the Gospel miracles are in two important respects entirely dissimilar.

XVII

In the first place, the evidence for the lives and doings of our Lord and His Apostles is infinitely better, and nearer in time to the facts, than the evidence for the doings of Moses and Elijah. I cannot stay to elaborate this thesis, but I may venture to remind you of Mr. Addis's essay in the *Studies in the Synoptic Problem*, in which this fact is brought out with great vividness and cogency. (I must observe, in passing, that—daring though it may seem to challenge an opinion expressed by you on a matter of New Testament criticism—I am not at all prepared to confine the term ' first-class New Testament evidence ' solely to the ' evidence of St. Paul's Epistles '. I must needs claim the major portion of the Synoptic Gospels, and the Acts of the Apostles, as ' first-class evidence ', not to mention the narrative parts of the Fourth Gospel.) I think it is not unreasonable to contend that, given the *a priori* possibility of miracles, the probability of the ' mythological explanation ' of any alleged miracles varies in direct proportion to the distance between the facts and the narratives. In other words—given the *a priori* possibility of miracles—the nearer the records are to the facts, the less likely the mythological explanation becomes. And, whilst I should not maintain that this consideration, by itself, reduced the probability of the ' mythological hypothesis ' in the case of New Testament miracles to vanishing point, or ruled it out altogether, I do think that it clears the ground very considerably for the ' historical hypothesis ' (i. e. the hypothesis that the facts actually happened as related).

Perhaps I may put it in this way. If I looked at the Gospel miracles without presuppositions of any kind, I might still feel unable to decide definitely between the ' historical ' and the ' mythological ' hypotheses : I might still be constrained, as I have said before, to remain in a position of agnosticism, or suspended judgement. But I should still feel that, inasmuch as the New Testament records are very considerably nearer in time to the facts which they relate than the Old Testament records, the ' historical ' hypothesis had a much greater chance of being true in the case of any one New Testament miracle than in the case of any one Old Testament miracle.

Of course, I should not in any case place all the miracles of the New Testament upon the same level, in regard to their claims upon the belief of Christians. For it is the case that, out of all the miracles recorded in the Bible, three, and three only, are required by the Creeds—that is, by the authority of the undivided Catholic Church—to be *ex animo* believed and accepted. Given the following assumptions (1) a belief in the Incarnation, (2) the *a priori* possibility of miracles—of which, as I have said, I can only recognize one kind, or order, (3) the 'first-class' quality of the main body of the Synoptic Gospels—I should say that the 'historical explanation' of the Walking on the Sea became invested with a high degree of probability. I should say that the 'mythological explanation' of this incident, whilst still barely possible, was distinctly otiose and unnecessary. But I should not claim, even for this, quite the same degree of absolute and utter certitude which I should for the three crucial miracles—the Virgin Birth, the Resurrection, and the Ascension. This claim is grounded in the fact that these three wonders are rooted in the very tissue of historic Christianity, as I conceive it; they are bone of its bone, and flesh of its flesh: the full credit of the 'infallibility of the Church' has been irretrievably hypothecated on their truth. You will easily understand that, when I place in one scale of the balance what I must needs consider the extremely frail, conjectural, subjective, and precarious reasons for accepting the 'mythological explanation' of these things, and in the other scale my deep, passionate, and overwhelming conviction that God would not have allowed His Church to require (in such an imperious and uncompromising manner) from its members unfeigned assent to propositions which were not, in the highest and most inclusive sense of the word, *true*—it is the latter scale which descends, and the former that 'kicks the beam'.

XVIII

It is pleasant to pass from the subject of Miracles, upon which discussion seems to be interminable and the possibility of agreement not yet within sight, to a region in which the edges of the fissure that divides us seem to have been driven fairly close together—namely, to that of the divine guidance bestowed upon the Church in its work of defining Christian doctrine. Let me begin this part of my letter by putting together the points upon which agreement seems to have been reached.

1. With regard to the 'metaphysical' doctrines, which, I suppose, constitute the greater portion of the whole body of Church doctrine, we agree to distinguish between 'content' and 'form'.
2. We agree that the content in these cases is 'permanent and unchangeable' (your own words, used on p. 2).
3. We agree, further, that 'the Church of Christ has been divinely guided in its definitions of doctrine' (your last letter, p. 107)—that is, presumably, in selecting appropriate 'forms' for the embodiment of the contents in question.
4. Finally, we agree that, whether these 'forms' are 'unalterable' or not, the question of their alteration, or of the substitution of other forms for them, does not now arise, inasmuch as there is no one universally recognized philosophical system current to-day and not current in the earlier centuries of the Christian era (my first letter, p. 39; your last, p. 97).

This seems to represent the exact extent of our agreement, formulated in precise and prosaic statements. But I should like to add, in estimating the balance between agreement and divergence, a certain, less easily definable, unity of aim and sympathy, which comes out in such sentences as the following, which I quote from your last letter :

'I profoundly believe that a presentation of Christianity

146 *Form and Content in Christian Tradition*

is possible which shall be at once in strict and full continuity with the past and shall yet be in complete harmony with the most assured results of progressive science in the present' (p.105).

'I do not doubt that there is a like balance between the ideas of permanence and of change in the world of thought and belief. My aim is to maintain an equilibrium between the two sides' (p. 106).

'Our object is, not to lay down what we think ought to be or what ought not, but to describe as truthfully and exactly as possible what actually is' (p. 113).

I must not stay to enlarge upon this point, but it may be of interest to you, and assist in the process of mutual understanding, if I say that I can heartily subscribe to every word of these sentences. After all, our object is certainly the same, namely, to present orthodox Christianity[1] to the modern world in an intellectual form which will not involve unnecessary difficulties (*some* difficulties it must always involve). But if our goal is the same, and if our roads are identical for a good part of the journey thither, there is considerable hope that we may be able, sooner or later, to arrive at a working agreement with regard to the remainder.

I must now proceed to say a final word about our differences under this head. Before doing so, I should like briefly to comment on one section of your last letter (p. 106, line 14 ff.). My remark about the 'comfort', which may be derived from surrendering oneself to the broad deep river of historical Christianity, was an *obiter dictum*, not an argument. I should never dream of attempting to base the truth of orthodoxy upon its 'comfort'-producing qualities: though there may be no harm in pointing them out by the way. Nor do I see the precise application of your remarks about the Church of Rome (ibid.). So far as I recollect, I had not made

---

[1] I am justified in using this expression by the fact that on p. 19 you 'distinctly claim' not to be 'unorthodox'.

any reference, direct or indirect, to that body. When I spoke of 'orthodox', 'traditional', 'historical', or 'Catholic' Christianity, I meant the faith, practice, and worship of the undivided Catholic Church of the first thousand years, and nothing narrower or more limited. These are, perhaps, not very important points, but they are worth making for the sake of clearness.

XIX

I have now to say a final word about the points of difference which still remain. And the first of these will not, I hope, detain us long. It has to do with the question of the 'unalterability' of the *forms* in which the 'metaphysical' doctrines of the Church are at present, and have been for the last fourteen or fifteen centuries, clothed. The matter is not one of great practical importance, because (as noted above, in my list of points of agreement) there is now no one universally accepted philosophy into terms of which they could be translated. It is, in fact, a purely theoretical and speculative problem, which might be formulated as follows: Supposing that at some period in the future, before the end of the world, a single logical system is invented, and becomes universally accepted, in which the category of Substance and Attribute and the copula (see p. 28) are definitely transcended and superseded: will it then be permissible for Christian theologians to set about the work of translating orthodox dogma from terms of Substance, Attribute, Nature, and Person into terms of this new logic, whatever it may be? Of course, for me the supposition is an impossible one, because, as I have said before, the thought-forms, in which the content of the *Depositum Fidei* was enshrined by the Catholic Church of the first millennium, seem to me to be rooted in the structure of the human mind as such: and I cannot conceive the possibility of their ever being superseded, so long as we retain our present faculties, constituted as they are. But, if I am to suppose, for the sake of argument, that such a new logic was discovered, and became universally and unquestioningly accepted—I do not mind saying that, under those circumstances, I think that Christian theologians would be justified in endeavouring to translate the 'metaphysical' parts of the Faith into such hypothetical new terms : though I should add the proviso, firstly, that it would be incumbent upon them to see that none of the heavenly treasure was lost, in the process of transferring it from one set of vessels to another—that is, to exercise the most minute and jealous care to see that the essential *content* of the Deposit was in no way impaired or diminished by the change of form :[1] and secondly, that, until Ecumenical authority had had an opportunity of pronouncing upon the results of their labours, the new formulations would have to be regarded as purely speculative and provisional, and that, meantime, the old categories and the ancient creeds would have to be considered as holding the field.

Of course, this is a purely speculative, perhaps a fantastic, supposition, which may never be realized at all, which certainly no one now alive upon this earth is likely to see realized. But it may help the process of mutual comprehension if I say that (in order to meet you as far as I can) I am prepared to explain the term ' unalterable ', as applied to the ' metaphysical ' parts of the Creeds, in the following way : The ' metaphysical ' doctrines are inherently and absolutely unalterable (' permanent and unchangeable ') in respect of their *content* ; in respect of their *form*, they are *conditionally* unalterable, i. e. they cannot be altered unless and until some instrument, more perfectly adapted for describing

---

[1] A proviso which has been conspicuously not fulfilled by most modern attempts to translate the Doctrine of the Person of Christ from terms of ' substance ' and ' nature ' into terms of ' value '.

the mutual relations of Reals, than was the old logic, is discovered. And, even then, I should contend that the Deposit of Faith could only be lawfully retranslated into the new terms by the same authority which had previously translated it into the old, viz., by that of the Universal Church. But the discovery of such a new logic is such an inconceivably remote contingency that I do not feel it necessary for practical purposes always to insert the adverb 'conditionally' before the word 'unalterable', when referring to this subject: and I still retain my private opinion that this contingency is not merely inconceivably remote, but actually impossible.

On this point, therefore (if I am not being too optimistic), I am inclined to think that our differences have been reduced almost to vanishing point. Most doctrinal controversies in the early Church were terminated by the discovery of a formula which men of goodwill on both sides could accept, though not always with a minute and exact identity of meaning: I would suggest, as such a 'Union' formula, the following: 'The metaphysical doctrines of the Church are strictly unalterable as to their content: as to their form, they are unalterable for all practical purposes and so far as human prevision can at present reach.'

XX

These considerations, however, do not apply to the 'historical clauses' of the Creeds. With regard to them, I should contend that there are three, and only three, legitimate mental attitudes, viz. :

1. Frank acceptance of them as they stand.
2. Frank rejection of them as they stand.
3. Pure agnosticism, or suspension of judgement.

The attitude of 'freedom of apprehension', which you claim to occupy, and which does not appear to be identical with any one of the above three, I should maintain to be inadmissible in their regard. It seems to me that whatever 'freedom of apprehension' may be permissible in the case of the 'metaphysical' dogmas arises out of the fact that the content and the (present *de facto*) form have not always been associated, and that the form is relative to the structure of human thought. I dare say that in regard to these doctrines there must always be a small margin of variation in the individual apprehension and assimilation of them. But the class of propositions to which the 'historical clauses' of the Creeds belong seems to be one in which such a margin of variation cannot, from the nature of things, be admitted: they must, as I have said before, be either taken or left: and this for the following reasons.

The historical clauses *purport* to be statements of objective, external *facts*, occurring in the material or phenomenal world—the world which we apprehend through the medium of sense. There is no use in blinking this fact. The clause affirming the Virgin Birth states what purports to be a sheer physical fact—that the body of Jesus Christ was conceived by Mary without the usual physical antecedents. The article affirming the Resurrection states that the death of that Body on the Cross was not followed by the usual physical consequents. There can be no doubt that these clauses (purport to) describe (alleged) events in the material world: for our Lord's Body, whilst He lived on earth, certainly was part of the material world. Now I should contend that no proposition which purports to describe either a permanent state of, or a change in, the material world, can reasonably be styled 'relatively true' or 'relatively false'. All such propositions must, in the nature of things, be either *absolutely* true—that is, true for everybody and true for God, the all-seeing and all-wise—or absolutely false. Because the material world itself is not 'relative'. It exists outside us and independently of us. It is not a mere picture in our heads, or a state of our consciousness. And if the material world exists independently of us and absolutely, or in its own right, clearly also its various states, and the changes that occur in it, are absolute, and not relative— they are not created by us : they are what they are, whether we are there to see or not. Consequently, there is no element of ' relativity ' in such a statement as this, ' The earth goes round the sun'. This, we happen to know, is ' absolutely ' true. The earth, ever since the beginning of its separate existence, always has gone round the sun : it was in actual fact going round the sun, even when everybody believed that the sun was going round the earth. Similarly, there is no element of relativity in the contrary proposition, 'The sun goes round the earth'. This, we should say, is ' absolutely '—or quite independently of our perceptions or preferences—false. I imagine that even the wildest subjectivist would hardly assert that the sun moved round the earth until the time of Copernicus, and that the opposite has been the case ever since.

There are, it is true, a certain number of affirmations about the external world which might be described in a certain sense as infected with relativity : and these are affirmations in which the predicate has a numerical or quantitative determination. For instance, we might say that the proposition ' The London train leaves at 7.35 ' was ' relatively true ', even though the fact might be that it left at 7.33. We express the same idea in less philosophical language when we say that a proposition, which we know to be somewhat inexact or inaccurate, is ' near enough '. I suppose the instance which I have given above is said to be ' relatively true ' in the sense that it is true, or practically satisfactory, for the purposes of a man who is accustomed to allow himself at least ten minutes' margin for catching trains ; but it is clear that it would be false relatively to a man who made a point of arriving at the station not more than one minute before

152 *Form and Content in Christian Tradition*

the departure of his train. But in any case it is obvious that the clauses of the Creed which affirm the Virgin Birth and the Resurrection have no element of 'relativity' in them, in this sense. It would be absurd to say that such a startling assertion as that 'Jesus Christ had no human father' was 'inaccurate' or 'inexact'. No one would say that Dr. Cook's claims to have reached the North Pole were 'inaccurate', unless he were consciously indulging in jocular *meiosis*.

I am therefore still constrained to contend that in the case of the clauses affirming the Virgin Birth and Resurrection (*a*) form and content are coincident and inseparable, and that (*b*) even if, for the purposes of thought, we distinguish them, there is no trace of relativity in the *form* of these historical propositions, such as I have admitted to exist in the case of the metaphysical propositions. It follows, therefore, that, in regard to them, the claim to 'freedom of apprehension' or 'partial affirmation' cannot be conceded; as I said at the beginning of this section, the only attitudes which I can recognize as being logically legitimate are frank acceptance, frank rejection, and frank agnosticism. And, on this point at least, I think I can claim to have on my side whatever weight may be supposed to attach to the opinion of the 'plain man' or the 'man in the street'.

XXI

Perhaps, after all, by 'freedom of apprehension' you really mean what I have called 'agnosticism'—the attitude of neither affirming nor denying. But I must point out that, so far as its bearings on the question of the 'infallibility' or 'trustworthiness' of the Church are concerned, the third attitude, that of 'agnosticism', is practically equivalent to the second, that of 'rejection'. It is obvious that an attitude of 'agnosticism' or 'suspense of judgement', in regard to what is imperiously inculcated by a guide claiming to be 'infallible', argues a considerable degree of mistrust and absence of confidence in the said guide. We are, therefore, brought back to the second main point of difference under this head, viz. whether or not the 'divine illumination' which we both admit to have been bestowed upon the Church in the work of defining Christian doctrine was of such a degree of intensity that it can reasonably be described as endowing the Church with 'infallibility'. A few words must now be devoted to this question.

XXII

And first, with regard to the grounds on which this fundamental premiss of the 'infallibility of the Church' rests. In my first letter (p. 38) I based it frankly upon an 'intuition'. You, however, can only regard my claim to possess this intuition as involving a '*petitio principii* on a large scale' (p. 109). You had made this criticism already in your second letter (on pp. 52, 53), and I had retorted with a *tu quoque*, of which you candidly admit the force (p. 109). I do not know that there is very much more to be said on the subject, from the point of view of pure logic. In regard to dependence upon unproved and unprovable assumptions, we both, and all Christians with us, are 'in the same boat'; nor does it seem to me that the difference in the degree of definiteness with which we hold what is in reality one and the same fundamental principle (cf. pp. 61, 63) constitutes a ground for assuming one way of holding it to be valid, and the other not. The pot has no right to reproach the kettle with blackness, even though the kettle's integument may be of a somewhat more definitely raven hue than its own. Your remarks about 'anticipated truth' and 'verification' (p. 110) are, of course, from my point of view, unexceptionable. In fact, it seems to amount to a statement, in different words, of the principle which I ventured to expound on pp. 72, viz. that religious principles are given in the first instance by 'intuition' or the 'gift of Faith' (these are only names for the same ineffable fact, viewed respectively from man's side and from God's), and verified by the consciousness of the reception of 'grace', or spiritual help. For, how do you come by your 'anticipated truths', unless it be by direct, though unanalysable, revelation from God—that is, by a flash of divinely bestowed insight or intuition ? You would, I imagine, hardly say that you had stumbled upon them by pure accident, like Archimedes in his discovery of hydrostatics : and you would hardly maintain, in view of facts like the Messina earthquakes and the *Titanic* disaster (not to mention the present war), that the 'verification', even for such a proposition as 'God is love', was a matter of direct sensory observation. But it does not seem unreasonable to assert that whatever guarantee is afforded by 'intuition' on the one hand and moral and spiritual 'verification' on the other can be claimed as much by those parts of Catholicism which are peculiar to it as by those which it has in common with orthodox Protestantism ; and, indeed, you profess yourself willing 'to share with' me 'the benefit of these considerations': so that, perhaps, no more need be said upon this section of our argument.

XXIII

I welcome what you say in the footnote to p. 106: 'The weakened sense which you attribute to these words "infallibility", "unalterability" goes far to meet me,' despite the fact that in the text of your letter you describe them as 'unfortunate'. I should not, indeed, have, myself, described this sense as a 'weakened sense': I am not aware that any responsible person ever has attributed any other sense to the word 'infallibility' than that of 'incapacity for deceiving or being deceived': and I should have supposed it self-evident that, so far as the word 'unalterable' is applied to the Catholic Faith, it is only applied *simpliciter* to the essential 'content', as distinguished from the 'form' (cf. p. 23). However, we need not waste time in discussing this question. I am glad that I have succeeded in making clear to you exactly what I mean by the 'unalterability of the Faith' and the 'infallibility of the Church'. But I very much regret that I cannot see my way to oblige you by dropping these terms, as you suggest in the footnote quoted above. No doubt, the word 'infallibility' tends to arouse many prejudices in the minds of some people: it calls up visions of the Vatican Council of 1870, of Ultramontanism, Inquisitors, and thumb-screws. But I am afraid I cannot help that. It is sometimes necessary to adhere tenaciously to a particular word, despite its accidental unpopularity, because it is the only word which really expresses a particular meaning—as in the case of the *Homoousion*. And so it is in the present instance. We could not drop the *word* without appearing to disparage the idea: for there is no other term which exactly expresses what we mean.

XXIV

Perhaps, however, the process of replying to isolated points is somewhat unsatisfactory. It will be simpler if, at the cost of some prolixity, I venture to sketch the way in which I arrive at my position as a whole, replying to any further points of difference as they emerge in the course of the discussion.

I find myself in need of a religion; that is, of some means of access to God, some means of obtaining help from Him towards salvation from sin, and some reliable information about Him. For various reasons, which I need not go into here, Buddhism, Mohammedanism, Bahaism, and so forth, do not satisfy me. Christianity, therefore, holds the field, in default of other claimants. But, I no sooner state to myself 'I must be a Christian', than the question rises up in front of me, 'What is Christianity?' And, at first sight, it would seem reasonable to reply, 'Christianity is what the great majority of those who profess and call themselves Christians believe it to be'; in other words, what I have designated as 'Catholicism'; just as, if I were inquiring 'What is Radicalism?' it would be *prima facie* reasonable to reply 'Radicalism is what all, or most, persons who call themselves Radicals declare it to be'.

Let me insert at this point an anecdote which will illustrate the *prima facie* reasonableness of this provisional answer to the question.

I have a friend who is a devout and learned member of the Jewish Church. Some time ago he had occasion to publish a pamphlet in which he addressed himself especially to the consideration of the question 'What is the essence of Judaism?' The course of his argument compelled him to make use of analogies drawn from Christianity, and in one section of his treatise he found himself referring to the doctrine of the Real Presence as 'one of the central doctrines of Christianity'. For this, he was somewhat vehemently attacked by certain Christian divines, who shall be nameless, on the ground that the doctrine in question was not a central doctrine of Christianity, but merely of one type, and that the least enlightened and progressive type, of Christianity. To which my friend, very reasonably in my opinion, replied, 'Your special beliefs and preferences, or those of *English* Christians in particular, have nothing to do with me; no more have your views as to what constitutes "progress". I stand outside Christianity altogether; religiously, and to a certain extent socially, my outlook and environment are cosmopolitan rather than insular; I therefore view Christendom as a whole, in the character of a detached and dispassionate observer. Moreover, I am not specially interested in its origins; for my purposes, I only need to take cognizance of the state in which it is now, and has been for by far the greater part of its history. Consequently, I feel myself entitled to assume that "Christianity" is what the vast majority of its adherents declare it to be ; and my statement about "the Real Presence" was, therefore, perfectly correct.'

It is, perhaps, not uncharitable to suppose that the divines in question had, hitherto, tacitly assumed as a matter of course that 'Christianity' was mainly identical with Anglo-Saxon, or possibly with Teutonic Christianity, and that Christianity as it exists in other than Teutonic countries was comparatively negligible. I need not point out to you how intensely *borné*, provincial, and insular such a view appears, if formulated in express terms. But, for any one who rejects it, as the philosopher, the 'spectator of all time and all existence', necessarily must, the only attitude possible at the beginning of the quest, would seem to be that of my Jewish friend, 'I assume provisionally that "Christianity" is what the overwhelming majority of Christians say that it is'.

I do not, of course, assert that this consideration possesses anything like absolute cogency ; its only value, so far, is that it gives me an ἀφορμή for my inquiry. Aristotle (*Top.* 100 a 29) says that dialectical reasoning necessarily starts from τὰ ἔνδοξα, 'current opinions', which he proceeds to define as the opinions held by 'all men', 'the majority of men', or by 'the wise'. I do not think it is too much to claim this proposition ('The presumption is that "Christianity" in the strict sense = "Catholicism"') as an ἔνδοξον, vouched for by a sufficient number of σοφοί, to serve as a starting-point for my research.

Perhaps this idea might be expressed in the following way. Imagine a Martian, or some completely impartial visitant from another world, studying the present state of Christianity, in order to arrive at a comprehension of its essential nature and meaning. Undoubtedly at first sight the most massive and imposing fact which would force itself upon his attention would be the existence of a great central block numbering some four hundred millions of people (that is, nearly four-fifths of the total periphery of Christendom), which, with whatever cleavages of external unity and diversities of rite and custom, holds and believes in what is substantially the same conception of the Christian religion. Throughout the whole length and breadth of this block there runs a single threefold grain or structure—doctrinal, institutional, and sacramental. The Nicene Creed, the great doctrines of the Trinity, the Incarnation, and the Atonement, the threefold ministry, the sacraments, the 'Communion of Saints': these things are the same in Moscow as they are in Paris, the same in Siberia as they are in Galway. He would notice, on the other hand, when looking at what I may, without disrespect, call the 'fringe' which surrounds this great central block, that the various comminuted fragments, of which the fringe is made up, have all, at one time or another, been broken off from the main block; and that they do not seem to have any one clearly essential principle binding them together, other than that of their separation from it. He would notice, further, that so far as they have any positive structure at all, it is identical with that of the main block, only cut down and mutilated in varying degrees of completeness. Some which lie close to the main block have the three-fold grain very clearly marked: others have it less distinctly visible, and in others it has been almost entirely obliterated. Those which lie farthest away, on the extreme edge of the fringe (the schools of thought associated with the names of Troeltsch and Jatho), seem to shade off into and to be practically indistinguishable from the surrounding abyss of pure agnosticism. At first sight, then, it seems probable that the central block really is what it claims to be, namely, real or essential Christianity, and that the fringe consists of defective, mutilated, or cut-down versions of it.

If, however, I interrogate the various sections of the fringe as to their own *raison d'être*, I find that they all return pretty much the same reply. All claim that the great central block consists of a kernel of genuine Christianity, which has been coated over in the course of ages with a thick crust of non-Christian accretions. I find, indeed, that the non-Catholic bodies are not at all unanimous in their replies to the question, ' Which Catholic doctrines or practices belong to the kernel, and which to the adventitious crust ? ' Some, for instance, would say that such ideas as the Real Presence and Communion of Saints belonged to the ' crust ', but that the doctrines of the Trinity and the Incarnation belonged to the ' kernel '. Others would say that the whole three-fold structure which I have noted above belonged to the ' crust ', and that the ' kernel ' consisted merely of monotheism and morality, or of morality only. Nor is there any unanimity as to when the alleged process of ' accretion ' began ; some place its beginning at the end of the ' first six centuries ', some immediately after the fourth, some after the first. I have, therefore, to look into history, to examine the origins of Christianity for myself, and to form my own judgement as to whether or not Catholicism is real Christianity, or real Christianity *plus* a ' crust ' of paganism.

I find, as a result of my historical investigations, that Catholicism can be traced back, in essentials, at least to the last quarter of the second century A.D. Beyond this point, indeed, the evidence becomes fragmentary and imperfect ; but, so far as I can pierce the mists which involve the primitive beginnings of Christianity, I seem to see the characteristic lines of Catholicism running back through Irenaeus, Polycarp, and Ignatius, into the apostolic age and joining up there with the main tendencies of the preaching of St. Paul and St. John. (I am speaking, of course, in the most summary fashion, and have not time or space to prove all these historical assertions here.) I need not remind you of what scholars like Kirsopp Lake say about Pauline sacramentalism and Johannine mysticism. But, even so, I am not yet out of the wood. Even if it be admitted that Catholicism is the legitimate continuation and development of Pauline sacramentalism, it would not necessarily follow that it was the legitimate development of authentic Christianity—that is, of Christianity as taught by Christ. For there is always the hypothesis, on which liberal Protestantism is being more and more forced back, that St. Paul and St. John (doubtless unconsciously and with the best of motives) misrepresented the Founder of Christianity. I have still to reckon with the theory which holds that through the medium of St. Paul and his Gentile converts, the characteristic ideas and usages of the Mystery Religions filtered into Christianity, and that the Apostle of the Gentiles was the first great corrupter of the primitive simplicity of the Gospel. There seem, in short, to be two possible hypotheses of the origin of Catholicism : (1) that it really is what it claims to be, the legitimate development and explication of a deposit committed by Christ to his followers ; (2) that it is a vast mass of Graeco-Roman accretion, walling in and concealing from view the original core of the Master's teaching, which is alleged to have been nothing but monotheism and morality, contained in the fantastic and delusive forms of Jewish apocalyptic.

From the purely intellectual point of view it seems to me that either of these hypotheses will fit, or, at any rate, can be made to fit, the facts ; and I do not know that on purely intellectual grounds I should ever be able to decide between them. Of course, the 'secularization-hypothesis' involves the rejection of certain parts of the Gospels (that is, of the only evidence which we possess for the life of Christ), as, for instance, the passages which represent the Founder of Christianity as speaking of ' My Church ', promising His Apostles that what they should bind on earth should be bound in heaven, and requiring the universal propagation of baptism : but the explanation which it provides for the existence of these passages, namely, that they are due to an unconscious coloration of the facts, in the minds of the Evangelic writers, by the incipient Catholicism of the Pauline school, is not in the nature of things impossible ; *a priori*, I should say that the ' secularization-hypothesis ' was no less, and no more, probable than the ' Deposit-hypothesis '. I find, in fact (if I may be allowed the use of a profoundly conventional metaphor), that I have come to the ' parting of the ways ', and there is no signpost to tell me whether to turn to the right hand or to the left. It is just at this point that some unseen power seems to take hold of me and push me forcibly down the left-hand road ; that is, the road of identifying myself with, and committing myself to, the great central mass of Christianity. This is what I meant by the phrase ' intuition '. It is not necessary for me here to discuss the exact nature of this ' intuition ', as a function of the soul ; I have really nothing more to add to what I said in my second letter (p. 62, l. 20). I am now only concerned to point out the exact place which it occupies in the process whereby I arrive at my position. My ' intuition ' simply shows me, in a perfectly general sense, that the left-hand road is to be taken ; in other words, that the great secular development of Catholic Christianity really was inspired by the Holy Spirit, and that ' historical ' or ' traditional ' Christianity—the Christianity of the great central block—is to be believed and accepted. I look at the venerable fabric of the historic Church and Faith, viewing it as an indissoluble whole, cohering together in unity and simplicity : and, despite the superficial disfigurements which man has been permitted to inflict upon it (such as the breaches of visible Church communion) and the adventitious growths which deform some parts of it (such as the one-sided development of the modern Papacy), I find myself saying ' Surely

God is in this place : this is none other than the house of God, and this is the gate of heaven '.

Of course, I quite admit that this 'intuition', or 'categorical imperative', constitutes a valid argument only for me and others who are conscious of it. I cannot really argue with any one who altogether repudiates possessing it, nor do I pretend to be able to prove to such a one that he ought to possess it. It is just the same in the case of ethics, or aesthetics ; the man who possesses the ethical or aesthetic sense could not argue with an opponent who disclaimed its possession, because there would be no common premisses from which the argument could start. And this discussion in which we have been engaged has only been rendered possible by the fact (as it seems to me) that you *do* possess this 'intuition' or 'categorical imperative', only, as I said on p. 74, in an imperfect or weakened form. I cannot *prove* to you that you ought to have this intuition in the same form in which I possess it, any more than Aristotle could prove to the possessor of an imperfect moral sense that he ought to have a perfect one.[1] In the nature of the case, all that I can hope to do is to show (a) that, *given* my premisses, my conclusions irresistibly follow (which, I gather, you do not dispute), and (b) that the objections sometimes raised against these premisses are not insuperable or unanswerable. And this, in the last resort, is all that any theologian, whatever religious system he may be defending, can pretend to accomplish. Were it otherwise—were it possible to *prove* propositions about God and heavenly things by direct induction from sense-observation, like the laws of natural science, or by direct deduction from the necessary laws of thought, like the truths of mathematics—there would be no such thing as divisions of religious opinion, on the one hand ; and there would be no room left for the exercise of the virtue of Faith, on the other.

[1] The best argument that Aristotle can find for dealing with the man who challenges fundamental moral principles is to inform him that he needs ' chastisement ' rather than ' demonstration '.

XXV

You will, no doubt, see from the foregoing what answer I should give to the criticism contained in the following words (p. 109 of your last letter) : ' I cannot in the least see that broad antecedent principles such as these (the ideas of God, Freedom, and Immortality) supply any sound analogy or justification for the claim that you make to take on trust an elaborate system consisting of a great number of distinct propositions.' I suppose your contention is, that there is no analogy from a simple ' intuition ' which gives a simple, single proposition, such as ' God exists ', to an alleged ' intuition ' which vouches for an elaborate system consisting of many propositions. But I must point out this : I do not claim to be able to hold the whole body of Catholic doctrine in the focus of attention simultaneously, and to have a simultaneous intuition of the truth of each and every particular member of it. I merely claim to see by intuition the truth, or the divinity, of ' historic Christianity '—that is, the Christianity of the ' great central block '—as an undifferentiated whole. I do not pretend to have sixty separate and synchronous intuitions assuring me that this, and this, and this detail of Catholicism is true. All I claim is to know by intuition that Catholicism in general is true. I begin with the whole, and work down through the process of reasoning and inquiry to the parts. It follows that what I should put forward as being, for me, the really clinching argument on the subject of, let us say, the Virgin Birth, might be roughly summarized as follows : ' Catholicism as a whole is true ; the Virgin Birth is an integral part of Catholicism ; therefore the Virgin Birth is true.' No doubt it is just here that you will find the *petitio principii.* You would, no doubt, contend that, by assuming the truth of Catholicism, I implicitly assume the truth of the Virgin Birth ; and am therefore begging the precise question at issue. But I may remind you that this *petitio principii,* if such it is to be called, is one which is implicit in the syllogism as such. The objections which have been raised, on this score, by modern logicians against the syllogism, as a form of reasoning, are well known. The stock instance is something as follows: We wish, let us say, to prove that Socrates is mortal; we therefore reason as follows: ' All men are mortal; now Socrates is a man; therefore, Socrates is mortal.' It is urged, with good reason, that the conclusion is really implicit in the major premiss. Therefore, it is contended, syllogistic reasoning is a perpetual revolution in a circle, which can never disclose to us any truth which we do not know already. I imagine that the usual reply to this difficulty would run somewhat in this manner: ' The psychological process, of which the syllogism is the logical formulation, is as follows: we have presented to us a single homogeneous whole or unity, which may be described as " humanity in general " ; and within it, but indissolubly rooted in it, we distinguish two elements or aspects, namely, " Socrates " and " Mortality ", which are seen to cohere together in virtue of their own co-inherence in the general mass of " humanity ".' Thus, all syllogistic reasoning is, in the last analysis, *a process of inspection*; and this is the point which I tried to make on page 64 in my second letter. ' Having obtained my principle by means of intuition (i.e. that " orthodox Christianity " is true) I can then proceed by way of pure ratiocination, *or rather of mere inspection of the facts*. I have only to inform myself as to what the truths of orthodox tradition actually are.' When we ' deduce ' a new truth from an old, what really happens is that we look, more attentively and minutely than we have *ex hypothesi* hitherto done, at the old truth: and, for the first time, discern the new truth contained or embedded in it. And so it is in the present instance. We have given to us, by Faith, the general belief that ' traditional Christianity ' is the authentic Deposit of truth, committed by our Lord to His Apostles, and faithfully preserved, according to the mind of God, by the Spirit-bearing Church ; we then look more closely into the heart of this great and venerable fact, ' traditional Christianity ', to which we have in a general sense committed ourselves ; and we find there, not only grace and help, but light and truth, expressed in a system of doctrines, each and all of which are guaranteed, for us, by their common co-inherence in the total fact of ' Catholicism '. Whatever may be thought of the general premiss from which it starts, I do not think that this procedure can really be impugned in respect of formal correctness.

Then, of course—when the believer has passed from the stage of *implicit* faith, in which he merely believes, in a general sense, that what the Church says is true, to that of *explicit* Faith, in which he accepts each and every detail of what is laid down as *de fide*—follows the process of ' moral and spiritual verification ', whereby the ' anticipated truth ', viz. that Catholic Christianity is to be absolutely trusted, is found in a thousand ways to be the key that fits into the lock of life's myriad perplexities and trials. But of this I have written above (p. 72), so that I need not enlarge upon it now.

XXVI

At this point, then, our discussion may close. In the nature of the case, it was not to be expected that either of us should decisively refute, or convert, the other ; but it is something that we have been able (as I think we have) to trace our surface differences in regard to certain beliefs down to divergences (happily, not very great or permanently irremediable divergences) in respect of fundamental and indemonstrable $\dot{\alpha}\rho\chi\alpha\acute{\iota}$. If I look back over the course of the debate, what seems to stand out in strongest relief is the fact that we seem to have come much nearer to an agreement on the question of the divine illumination bestowed on the Church by the indwelling of the Holy Spirit, than on the question of Miracles. Perhaps the reason for this is to be found in the fact that religion unites, whereas philosophy divides. Even in regard to the question of miracles, I can go with you in all your positive statements—as, for instance, when you say ' I was quite prepared for the presence in the universe of extraordinary forces, expressing themselves in extraordinary phenomena. I do not doubt at all that the public ministry of our Lord and of the Apostles was accompanied by such phenomena' (p. 100). It is only when you begin to philosophize upon miracles, to raise the question of their metaphysical *rationale*, and to formulate canons of conformity and nonconformity to ' the laws of matter and motion ' for determining their *a priori* possibility, that serious and radical divergences begin to make themselves felt. I do not, of course, suggest for a moment that it is wrong or undesirable to raise these philosophical questions in regard to Miracles : I am merely pointing out the obvious fact that, the deeper one plunges into the jungle of purely intellectual speculation, the farther away one tends to get from one's companions. Perhaps I may be permitted to emphasize this one point in conclusion : I think that, given an indefinite time for discussion, we might very well arrive at an agreement, which was for all practical purposes complete, on the abstract question of the ' divine guidance of the Church ' in the definition, at least, of the ' metaphysical ' doctrines. But (if I may venture, without offence, to say so) I cannot conceive myself ever under any circumstances accepting your distinction between *contra naturam* and *supra naturam* events, or admitting any really final and conclusive test of the *a priori* credibility of miracles other than that of conformity to what we know by revelation of the character of God.

However, I do not wish to end upon the note of divided opinion. I would rather conclude this letter, and our correspondence, in the spirit of hope—hope that, sooner or later, those who think with you will banish what I must needs consider the vain and illusory fear of 'contradicting scientific laws', and will see their way clear to taking just that little step forward which will bring them into line with the main army of orthodox Christians ; so that all together may at length set forth with the momentum of united millions, in the power of the everlasting Gospel, conquering and to conquer.

Believe me to be,

Very sincerely yours,

N. P. WILLIAMS.

www.ingramcontent.com/pod-product-compliance
Lightning Source LLC
Chambersburg PA
CBHW050808160426
43192CB00010B/1688